SPIRITUALISM VERSUS CHRISTIANITY.

A Fully Developed Medium Eighteen Hundred Years Ago.

See The Fortieth Page.

Spirits Exhilarate; Large Potations Intoxicate; Persistence Brutalizes.

"WE HAVE TO CONTEND AGAINST OUR OWN FANATICISM; FOR I ASSURE YOU, FROM MY OWN EXPERIENCE AND OBSERVATION, THAT THE FASCINATION OF THIS INTERCOURSE IS SO GREAT THAT ITS TENDENCY IS TO LEAD MEN AWAY FROM THEIR PROPER JUDGMENT, AND INSTILL A SPIRIT OF FANATICISM MOST REVOLTING TO THE CALM AND NATURAL MIND."—*Judge Edmond's Lecture, in the Broadway Tabernacle, N. Y., February Sixteenth, Eighteen Hundred and Fifty-Five.*

SPIRITUALISM

VERSUS

CHRISTIANITY;

OR,

SPIRITUALISM THOROUGHLY EXPOSED

BY

J. W. DANIELS,

"And when they shall say unto you,
Seek unto them that have familiar spirits,
And unto wizards that peep, and that mutter.
Should not a people seek unto their God?
For the living to the dead?"—Isaiah viii: 19.

"If they hear not Moses and the Prophets,
Neither will they be persuaded
Though one rose from the dead."—Luke xvi: 31.

"Add thou not unto his words,
Lest he reprove thee,
And thou be found a liar."—Proverbs xxx: 6.

NEW YORK AND AUBURN:
MILLER, ORTON & MULLIGAN.
NEW YORK: 25 PARK ROW.—AUBURN: 107 GENESEE ST.
1856.

J. J. REED,
PRINTER AND STEREOTYPER,
16 Spruce-St., N Y.

INTRODUCTION.

Spiritualism has been in operation in this country about seven years, during which, it has made rapid progress, owing to the fact that its character and influence have not been generally understood. Its adherents have organized a Society for the Diffusion of Spiritual Knowledge. The chief officers of this Society are as follows:

PRESIDENT.

Gov. NATHANIEL P. TALLMADGE, Wisconsin.

VICE-PRESIDENTS.

Chief Justice Joseph Williams, Iowa.
Judge Willie P. Fowler, Kentucky.
Judge R. P. Spaulding, Ohio.
Judge Charles H. Larrabee, Wisconsin.
Horace H. Day, New York.
Hon. Warren Chase, Wisconsin.
Dr. David Corey, Illinois.
Gen. Edward F. Bullard, New York.
Hon. Richard D. Davis, New York.
Dr. George T. Dexter, New York.
Major George W. Raines, U. S. A.
E. W. Bailey, Pennsylvania.
Phineas E. Gay, Massachusetts.

It seems very strange to us to see a professedly religious association headed by politicians, civilians and warriors! This should, doubtless, be imputed to our predilections for Christianity.

The New York Mirror aptly remarks, that in the "Association of Spiritualists just formed, with Ex-Governor Tallmadge as President, governors, senators, lawyers, merchants, and manufacturers figure exclusively. There is not so much as *one carpenter* or *fisherman* among them all."

GOVFRNOR TALLMADGE, in a letter accepting the Presidency of this society, says:

"Knowing the solid foundation on which 'The Society for the Diffusion of Spiritual Knowledge' is based, and that those engaged in it intend to spare no pains or means to advance the great objects for which it was instituted, I cannot fail to foresee and appreciate the grand results of its operations. * * Your society is the nucleus of mighty movements, which will in due time be fully developed. There are causes now operating which, with Spiritualism as the fulcrum, will, like the lever of Archimedes, move the world."

The Society says in its ADDRESS:

"Within the last two years, Spiritualism has increased in strength and stature, with a growth unprecedented in the history of mental giants. If it be a lie, there is every prospect of its enveloping this world, and, by its weight, sinking this world one degree lower in the depth of degradation. If it be a lie, it has come in so lovely a garb that men will seek it, unless they be warned by a strong voice; men will flee to it as though it were an angel sent from Heaven—will become enveloped in its false light, and will be borne down to death by the weight of its false glory. If it be a lie, ye men of America, who have one thought toward the good of your fellows, it is your duty to come forward as one man, to tear the veil from the face of the lie, and expose it in all its hideousness. We challenge you, as men—as earnest men, as men desiring the good of your fellows—to come forth and meet us in the fight, expose our errors, draw the shroud away, and enable the world to see us as we are. We challenge you to come and do that thing.

"We believe that Spirituality is a Heaven-born truth. We profess to know that angels from Heaven—that the Spirits of good men, progressing toward perfection—have come here upon the earth we stand on, and talked with us, face to face, and uttered words to us bearing the impress of their divine origin. We sincerely believe this. We are respectable men; we do not believe ourselves to be insane. We ask you to come and meet us, and discuss the question with us; to examine these facts which we allege, and to prove, if you are able, either that these facts never did occur, or that their origin is other than that which it purports to be.

"We come before you in this present shape to show you

to what a height the giant has attained. We come to you in this present shape to show you who are Spiritualists—the madmen in this world, who believe themselves to be the really clear-minded and sane men of this world. In this movement, which we have commenced, we believe we are the humble instruments in the hands of higher powers, for the production of great results. We are proud of the posts we occupy. We are not ashamed to present our names for your consideration. We are not ashamed to meet you on an equal platform, as men, and talk with you cerning this subject."

In a work published in this city, entitled "The Rappers," it is said: "In the city of New York, to which circle our personal investigation has been confined, there are, at the least calculation, forty thousand sincere believers in spiritual rappings. We cannot pretend to give the number of the disciples in the United States. The rush to consult the spirits, in both what are called private and public circles in New York, if known, would astound the public. From morning until noon, from noon until night, and from night until morning again, in parlors where flashing mirrors reflect rosewood, and velvet, and silver, and gold; in humble rooms where the floors and walls are bare, the tables are placed, and around them, men and women, with their hands spread out, and eyes fixed, as if on vacancy, are seated waiting for communications from the spirit-world."

The world should not be surprised by these "manifestations." They are nothing new. The history of Spiritualism is the history of *sorcery* in all ages. Egyptian sorcery furnishes the most remarkable antecedent to the present movement. The Spiritualism of the present was neither beyond the reach of the prophetic telescope nor the ken of Jehovah's prophets. The world has been premonished of its approach by the Seer of Patmos, the Apostle to the Gentiles, and the Saviour of the world. This fact is another evidence of the Divine origin of the book against which Spiritualism is arrayed, and which is the most formidable obstacle to its progress. Spiritualism proves itself to be *the* anti-christian movement of the present age, and one of the worst delusions which has ever afflicted the world. But it is not all to be met by sneers and cries of "humbug," "ventriloquism," "collusion," and "cheat." Intelligent men, learned men, and strong men, are conscientiously wedded to the system. Some of them have challenged the world to "meet them in the fight and expose their errors." It is no more than just that they should be met with candor and fairness. Every work which has been published, denying the alleged spiritual agency, has failed to meet the case, both in fact and in the estimation of the public. No work in which the agency of spirits has been admitted, has been sufficiently extensive to expose the evils of the system—evils which are much to be deplored. Being in possession of important facts, some of which had never been published, and others never in a connected form, we concluded to accept the "challenge." Hence this effort to expose the system and its evils, so antagonistic to Christianity.

There can be but two questions on this subject, in the mind of any person who is thoroughly acquainted with the phenomena.—First, the character of the spirits, and Second, the justice and propriety of holding intercourse with them.

These questions we have endeavored to meet. The whole subject has been thoroughly examined in the light of the Scriptures, profane history, and the developments of these times. Waving all cases of mere pretence—of which, doubtless, there have been many—we grapple with the real merits of the subject; and while we freely admit the reality of many of the manifestations, and that the phenomena are utterly inexplicable on any other hypothesis than that of spiritual agency, we prove that, to whatever other source this movement may be imputed, it is not the work of God, of holy angels, nor departed saints. We deem the intercourse sinful, fascinating, deceptive and very dangerous.

We prayerfully submit the result of our investigations to an indulgent and candid public. Should this work be the means of guarding some persons against "seducing spirits and doctrines of demons," and turning others from broken cisterns to the fountain of living waters, the hopes of the author will have been realized.

J. W. DANIELS.

NEW-YORK, *January*, 1856.

CONTENTS.

CHAPTER IV.

MODERN PHENOMENA ARE NOT PRODUCED BY HOLY ANGELS.

CHAPTER V.

SPIRITUALISM IS NOT THE WORK OF DEPARTED SAINTS.

CHAPTER VI.

EVIL CHARACTER OF THE SPIRITS.

CHAPTER VII.

SPIRITUALISM IS A REVIVAL OF SORCERY.

CHAPTER VIII.

THE BOOK OF THE PROPHETS OF THE SPIRITUALISTS.

CHAPTER IX.

ANCIENT ORACLES OF THE SPIRITUALISTS.

CHAPTER X.

SATANIC AND DEMONIAC MIRACLES.

CHAPTER XI.

SPIRITUALISM IS REVIVING POLYTHEISM.

CHAPTER XII.

PRETENDED ANIMATION OF A DIVINING IMAGE.

CHAPTER XIII.

CREED OF THE SPIRITUALISTS.

CHAPTER XIV.

THE EVILS OF SPIRITUALISM.

CHAPTER XV.

THE WORK OF SPIRITUALISM IS ANTI-CHRISTIAN.

CHAPTER I.

MODERN MANIFESTATIONS.

"They are the spirits of devils, working miracles, which go forth to the kings of the earth and of the whole world."—Rev. xvi: 14.

THE spirits commenced their manifestations in this country by knocking on the door of a house occupied by Mr. Michael Weekman, in Hydesville, in the town of Acadia, Wayne County, N. Y., in 1847. Mr. Weekman says, that one evening, about the time of retiring, he heard a rapping on the outside door. On opening it, he found no one there. He went in, for the purpose of retiring, and just before getting into bed, heard the rapping repeated. He quickly opened the door, went out and looked around, but found no one. It being frequently repeated, he took hold of the door-latch, and as soon as the knocking was repeated, he sprang out, went round the house, but no one could be found.

One night, a little girl, about eight years old, was heard to scream, the family ran to her, and as soon as she was able to relate facts, she said she felt something like a hand on the bed and all over her, but was not alarmed till it touched her face. It felt cold. It was some days before she recovered her equanimity.

The next family who resided in the house was that of Mr. J. D. Fox. Both Mr. and Mrs. Fox were members of the M. E. church, well known, and of unimpeachable character. They moved into the house where Mr. Weekman had lived, in December, 1847, and in March, 1848, first heard the noise. The knocking was so strong as to jar the floor. It was first heard one night, just after the family, except Mr. Fox, were in bed. It continued till they went to sleep, and they were unable to detect the cause. From that time it was continued each night. The 31st of March, the family retired early, and soon heard the knocking. A little girl, twelve years old, endeavored to imitate it, by snapping her fingers, and a response was given by knocking as many times as she snapped. When she stopped the sounds ceased. Another girl said, "Now do as I do," and began to strike one hand with the other; the knocks were repeated as before.

When intelligence was thus manifested Mrs. Fox requested it to count ten: it did so, by rapping ten times. It also, by request, counted the ages of the children correctly. Mrs. Fox questioned it as to its identity. When asked if it was a human being, it was silent. "Are you a spirit?" Two raps were given. "Are you an injured spirit?" Two raps, as before, were given. It was finally ascertained that it purported to be the spirit of a pedlar, who had been murdered in that house for his money—five hundred dollars—at the age of thirty-one ; and that he had left a wife and five children, and his wife had been dead about two years. The neighbors were then, by consent of the spirit, called in, and the questions continued.

From this family the manifestations have spread all over the United States and the Canadas.

It is said the spirits communicate by rapping, table tipping, writing through a medium, writing without a medium, speaking through a medium, and speaking without a medium.

Mediums are distinguished as rapping, tipping, writing, speaking, drawing, impressional, dreaming, and seeing mediums. The seeing and speaking mediums are deemed to be the highest order. Such are "seers" and "inspired" speakers.

JUDGE EDMONDS says, in the introduction to his work on spiritualism :

"I have known a pine table, with four legs, lifted up bodily from the floor, in the centre of a circle of six or eight persons, turned upside down, and laid upon its top at our feet, then lifted up over our heads, and put leaning against the back of the sofa on which we sat. . . . . I have seen a mahogany centre-table, having only a centre leg, and with a lamp burning upon it, lifted from the floor, at least a foot, in spite of the efforts of those present, and shaken backward and forward, as one would shake a goblet in his hand. . . . . I have known a dinner-bell, taken from a shelf in a closet, rung over the heads of four or five persons in that closet, then rung round the room over the heads of twelve or fifteen persons in the back parlor, and then borne through the folding-doors to the further end of the front parlor, and then dropped on the floor. I have known persons pulled about, with a force which it was impossible for them to resist; and once, when all my strength was added, in vain, to that of one thus affected. I have known a mahogany chair thrown on its side, and moved swiftly back and forth on the floor, no one touching it, through a room where there were, at least, a dozen people sitting. Yet no one was touched, and it was repeatedly stopped within a few inches of me, when it was coming with a violence which, if not arrested, must have broken my legs. . . . . My most secret thoughts—those which I never uttered to mortal man or woman—have been freely spoken, as if I had uttered them. I have known Latin, French and Spanish words spelled out through the rappings; and I have heard mediums, who knew no language but their own, speak in those languages, and in Italian, German and Greek, and in other languages unknown to me, but which were represented to be Arabic, Chinese and Indian, and all done with the ease and rapidity of a native. I have heard a person who knew nothing of music, except a little that he had learned at a country singing-school, go to the piano and play in perfect keeping, as to time and concord, the several parts of an overture to an opera."

WRITING AND TABLE BREAKING.

Extract from a letter from Thomas Neibert, of Natchez, Miss., to Gov. Tallmage:

"We have had rapped out: 'Lay fifty pieces of paper in a locked cupboard, and we will write on them.' In less than half an hour there was a communication of at least ten lines on each piece, and each communication perfectly characteristic of the individual professing to communicate.

"We have the remains of a table, all broken to pieces, by a spirit professing to be Samson. No person was near it. The table being near the wall, commenced moving as we came into the room to form a circle, and moved until it came to about the middle, when the spirit commenced breaking it; and the floor, when he got through, was a perfect sight to behold—all covered with splinters. The whole company, some ten or fifteen, all skeptics except myself, were perfectly convinced."—*Epitome of Spirit-intercourse*, p. 102.

AERIAL TRANSPORTATION.

Mr. John Quincy Adams, of Ohio, was returning from an absence, "when within about four miles of home, traveling on foot upon a turnpike, when he came to a 'bye-path,' which he took, as it was a nearer way home than the main road. After he had followed this path about three hundred yards (it was then between sundown and dark) he was, by an invisible power, lifted from the ground and carried though the air over the path, homeward, with such astonishing rapidity that he was unable to count the panels of a fence along which he was carried, and which he was impressed to number. He was transported thus nearly a mile. While he was being carried, a hand-saw and a square, which he held in his hands, were beaten together, and a delightful tune rang out. A brilliant light, apparently about four feet in circumference, shone out a short distance before him as he glided through the air."—*Spiritual Telegraph*, July 19, 1855.

A WRESTLING SPIRIT.

"Several friends had come together to witness the strange power that seemed to be at work at the house of brother J. A. While the rapping was going on, one of the company denounced the whole thing—said he did not believe it was spirits; or if it was, they could not rap and move tables, etc. He defied and dared the spirits, saying he could throw down or whip any spirit. The Doctor then inquired of the spirit that was rapping at the time, if he could wrestle; he said he could. He then asked if he was willing to wrestle and show fight with that gentleman; he said he was. The brave man then told the spirit to follow him out into the yard, and started, all the circle rising from the table, when it commenced moving towards the man, and hit him several hard blows before he reached the door, which hastened his steps; and as he passed out the table was thrown at him, only missing him a little, striking the door-facing about midway, denting and scaring the facing, bursting off the top of the table, breaking the legs, and leaving indentations as though bullets and shot had been fired into it.

"When the spirit-fighter had reached the yard he began striking, jumping as though he was contending with flesh and blood, manifesting all the signs of determined bravery to fight it out to the last. He was several times thrown hard on the ground, then struggled and regained his feet, and down he would come again. This mode of testing the invisible continued until the spirit's adversary was sorely wounded and worried out of breath and strength. He finally regained his foothold, made a hasty retreat into the house, up a flight of stairs, and taking to himself a private room, closed the door after him, declaring he never wanted to fight spirits any more, and that if they would let him alone he would them.—S. D. Page, Purdy, Ohio, June 19, 1853."—*Telegraph Papers*, vol. 2, p. 72.

PALACES OF THE SPIRITS.

According to Mr. Partridge, of the *Telegraph*, some of the most remarkable manifestations have occurred in Milfield, Athens county, Ohio. The family of Mr. Jonathan Koons had been holding intercourse with the spirits, when one night they made such a noise about his house that the family were afraid it would be torn down over their heads. Mr. Koons directed his son to go to the table, and take a pencil and paper and find out "what the devils wanted." The spirits requested that an "Electrical Table" should be made for their use. Subsequently the table was commenced according to their directions; but as its machinery proved defective, Mr. Koons determined to destroy it, when "frightful noises were again heard about his house, resembling the falling of trees, sometimes upon the roof of his dwelling, and sounds as if logs were rolled over it, and falling heavily upon the ground. His furniture was also moved about fearfully as before."

"The table was finally completed. The spirits then demanded that a variety of musical instruments should be procured. The instruments were purchased and placed around the table as the spirits ordered. The presiding genius called his name *King*. He said he had lived on this earth, 14,500 years ago, and had been acquainted, as a spirit, with Moses and the prophets, Christ and the Apostles.

"After these things were arranged they heard human voices, but could not distinguish words. The sounds appeared like shrieks, except at times they would attempt to speak through the harmonica, and then they could distinguish words. The spirits requested them to obtain a tin horn two feet long, two inches in diameter at the large end and one-eighth of an inch at the smallest part near the mouth. Through this horn the spirits speak audibly, so as to be plainly understood. They say this horn facilitates articulation, in helping to compress the atmosphere or direct the forces necessary to the utterance.

"The spirits requested them to build a room which is about eighteen by fifteen feet, and about nine feet high. This is built of logs with mud between, in the way that the cabins at the west are usually constructed. There is one door and one window in it. When these are closed the room is dark. The electrical table is placed at one end of the room, leaving space sufficient for a person to pass behind it. In the other end of the room there are several tiers of seats running entirely across the room, rising one above the other. There is a round table placed near the centre of the room, in front of this electrical machine, and between it and the audience. Upon this table, instruments, paper and pencils are placed, and with these the spirits play and write.

"Another room has been erected and similarly arranged by spirit direction, by Mr. John Tippie, some three miles from Mr. Koons, at which place similar manifestations occur.

"I attended three public circles in the spirit-house of Mr. Koons, and three in the spirit-house of Mr. Tippie; they are situated about three miles apart; the rooms and manifestations are very similar, although the electrical tables, so called, differ somewhat in their construction; the presiding spirits are of the same name, King; they claim to be father and son.

"These rooms will seat about twenty-five or thirty persons each, and are usually full. Many times, while I was there, more persons desired to go in than the house would hold, and some of them had to remain outside. They could hear the music and the spirits' conversation just as well. They only had to forego being touched by spirits and seeing them. The music is heard, under favorable circumstances, at the distance of one mile, or as far as any band of martial music can be heard. After the circle is formed, the door and window are shut, the light is usually extinguished, and almost instantaneously a tremendous blow with the large drumstick is struck on the table, when immediately the bass and tenor drums are beaten rapidly, like calling the roll no the muster-field, waking a thousand echoes. The rapid and tremulous blows on these drum are really frightful to many persons. This beating of the drums is continued five minutes or more, and when ended, King usually takes up the trumpet and salutes us with "Good evening, friends," or something like it, and often asks what particular manifestations are desired. If none are specially asked for, King often asks Mr. Koons to play on the violin, the spirit-band playing at the same time on the drums, triangle, tambourine, harp, accordeon, harmonica, etc., etc.; upon these the spirits perform scientifically, in very quick and perfect time. They commence upon each instrument at one instant, and in full blast, and stop suddenly after sounding the full note, showing that they have some more perfect method than we have of notifying each performer of the instant to start and stop. After the introductory piece on the instruments, the spirits often sing. I heard them sing. They spoke to us, requesting us to remain perfectly silent. Presently we heard human voices singing, apparently in the distance, so as to be scarcely distinguishable; the sounds gradually increased, each part relatively, until it appeared as if a full choir of human voices were in our small room, singing most exquisitely. I think I never heard such perfect harmony; each part was performed with strict attention to its relative degree of sound or force. . . . . I don't know that the spirits attempted to utter words with their song; if they did, they succeeded in this particular no better than modern singers. But it was hardly necessary for the spirits to articulate, for every strain and modulation seemed pregnant with holy sentiments, and language could scarcely signify more. After this vocal performance, several pieces of quick music were performed by spirits on the several instruments. They play faster than mortals generally do, and in most perfect time throughout. If any instrument gets out of chord, they tune it; they tuned the violin in my presence, and did it rapidly and skillfully. . . .

"Spirits' hands and arms were reörganized in our presence, on several of these occasions; and that we might see them more distinctly they sometimes wet their hands with a weak *solution of phosphorus*—which Mr. Koons prepared some time previous by their request—which emits a light so that their hands can be almost as distinctly seen in a dark room as they could be if the room were lighted. At one of these circles which I attended, there were three hands which had been covered with this solution of phosphorus, and we all saw them passing swiftly around the room, over our heads, carrying the instruments, and playing upon the violin, accordeon, triangle, harmonica and tambourine, and all keeping perfect time. These instruments were moved so swiftly and near the faces of the audience—our own among them—that we felt the cool atmospheric current as distinctly as we do that produced by a fan. Several of the company in different parts of the room remarked that they not only felt this disturbance of the air, but heard it, and distinctly saw the hand and instrument pass close to their faces. Several of us requested the spirits to place these instruments in our hands, or touch us on our heads or other parts of our bodies; and in most cases it was instantly done. I held up my hands, and requested the spirits to beat time with the tambourine on my hands. They did so, and gave me more than I asked for, by striking my knees, hands and head in a similar manner. I have seen the tambourine players in the minstrel bands in New York; I have seen the best performers in the country; but they cannot perform equal to these spirits. The perfect time, and the rapidity with which they beat, is truly surprising.

"Spirit-hands with phosphorous upon them passed around the room, opening and shutting, and exhibiting them in various ways and positions, which no mortal hand could assume or occupy—demonstrating them to be veritable spirit-hands, physically organized. The phosphorescent illumination from these hands was so distinct, that it occurred to me I could see to read by it; and I took a pamphlet from my pocket, and asked the spirit to place the hand over it, that I might see if I could read by the light. The spirit did so, when I at once perceived that I held the pamphlet wrong end up. I turned it, and could read. The members of the circle remarked that they could see very plainly my hands, face, and the pamphlet I held, and as distinctly could see the spirit's hand and a portion of the arm. I then put out my hands, and asked the spirits to shake hands with me; they did so almost instantly. I then asked them to let me examine their hands; and they placed them in mine, and I looked at them and felt them until I was entirely satisfied. Others asked the same favor, and it was readily granted them. These spirit-hands appeared to be reörganized from the same elements that our hands are; and, except that they had a kind of tremulous motion, and some of them being cold and death-like, we could not by our senses distinguish them from hands of persons living in the form.

"The spirit-hand took a pen, and we all distinctly saw it write on paper which was lying on the table; the writing was executed much more rapidly than I ever saw mortal hand perform; the paper was then handed to me by the spirit, and I still retain it in my possession. At the close of the session the spirit of King, as is his custom, took up the trumpet and gave a short lecture through it—speaking audibly and distinctly, presenting the benefits to be derived, both in time and eternity, from intercourse with spirits, and exhorting us to be discreet and bold in speech, diligent in our investigations, faithful to the responsibilities which these privileges impose, charitable towards those who are in ignorance and error, tempering our zeal with wisdom; and finally closing with a benediction.

"I am aware that these facts so much transcend the ordinary experience of mortals, that few persons can accept them as true on any amount of testimony. I obtained the address of the following named persons, and hope they will excuse me for the liberty I take in referring to them in this connection, for the confirmation of my statements. They were present at some or all the circles which I attended, when these manifestations occurred: R. I. Butterfield,

Cleveland, Ohio; William D. Young, Covington, Ind.; George and David Brier, Rainsville; Ind., David Edgar and daughter, Mercer county, Pa.; S. Van Sickles, Delaware, O.; S. T. Dean, Andrew Ogg, George Walker, and son, Amesville, O.; Azel Johnson, Milfield, O.; W. S. Watkins, New York; Thomas Morris and wife, Dover, O.; Dr. George Carpenter, Athens, O.; Thomas White, Mount Pleasant, O. Many other persons were present, whose names I did not learn.—CHARLES PARTRIDGE."—*Spiritual Telegraph, July* 7, 14, 21, 1855.

SPIRITUALISM IN CHINA.

The Overland China Mail of June 6, 1854, contains an account of spirit-manifestations in China, by Dr. Macgowan, of Ningpoo.

He says they have had the table tippings, or rather whirlings, and spirit-writings there for a long time. Writing is performed with a pencil or a chopstick, on a table which has been covered over thinly with bran, flour, dust or any powder to receive the communications.

"In a great number of cases the characters thus traced will be found in perfect accordance with the best style of composition, accurately communicating things altogether unknown to the operators.

"There is probably not a native living—Pagan or Christian, Jew or Mahomedan, or anything else, who does not religiously believe it to be owing to supernatural agency; and in support of that belief, almost any of them will give narratives, which, to say the least, must be admitted to be extremely curious; for, say they, if you invoke the presence of a ghost by suitable religious ceremonies, you will almost invariably have characters traced on the table by a spirit, which generally reveals something occult and mysterious.

"Mr. Li is now a fugitive, in danger of losing his head in consequence of revelations the *Kwei* or demons made to him a few months ago, respecting a new aspirant to the throne of this empire. Three of his accomplices were beheaded a few days since for the part they took in the affair!! We can imagine that some occidental practitioners of the art will claim superiority over their colaborators in the far east, averring that they call up at pleasure the names of Bacon, Franklin, and other sages; and, as one writes with delectable naïvete, possessing the ability to consult departed greatness, 'from a royal duke down to an American President!' Very well! The Chinaman is not a whit behind you in that respect. To select a single illustration—it may be found in Morrison's Dictionary: In 1814, a deposed officer of government was condemned to death for publishing an answer, which he declared, he had received in this way from Confucius. The purport of the answer was, that the Emperor should depute a prince to worship at the tombs of his ancestors, instead of going himself; and that the title of 'Emperor' should be taken from the demigod KWAN-TI—

ideas which were declared to breathe the most daring impiety. The government commonly discourages the practice.

"Soon after our arrival in NINGPOO, in 1843, such a wonderful impulse was suddenly given to the custom that it could only be compared to the prevalence of an epidemic. There was scarcely a house in which it was not practiced, for a season, almost daily. The cause of this remarkable revival of an old custom could not be ascertained; *but its subsidence, after a short period, was explained by the amount of mischief occasioned by those who followed or confided in the communications from Hades, and by the complaint that little real advantage ever accrued from this form of divination.*

"A club of literary graduates were in the habit of assembling in a Tanist temple for practising the KI, as the ceremony is called; and many and marvellous are the revelations told of the 'spiritual manifestations' which they elicited. It was continued for a long time, until the arrival of an intendant, who disproved of the demonaltry; he addressed the party as a friendly adviser, urging the discontinuance of such practices, on the ground that he *had never known any good, but considerable evil to result from them.* His counsel was followed; and since that time this sort of divination has been tried only occasionally, and by individuals.

"A poor graduate, after worshiping and employing incantations, invoked the presence and instructions of his deceased grandfather: whereupon the pencil traced, in a legible hand, some suggestions, which were complied with, *but which proved disastrous to the scholar.*"

DR. DEXTER, in his introduction to "Spiritualism," says, "my youngest daughter—scarcely nine years of age—became visibly agitated all over—her countenance changed, and she was evidently resisting, with considerable effort, what I supposed a slight attack of illness from being so long shut up in one room. I asked her if she was sick. She replied, "No, but I cannot keep either my body or my hands still. I am trembling all over." As soon as she uttered these words, her hands and arms were violently shaken. * * * * She became very much alarmed, and, running to her mother, who was also deeply moved at this unlooked-for manifestation, she said, while her voice trembled with fear, "O, mother, take me away!—take me away!" But her arms were forcibly wrested, as it were, from her mother's neck, and thrown violently up and down. * * * Being fatigued, about one o'clock, she was ordered, by the spirits, to leave the circle; and, not immediately complying with this direction, her chair was drawn from under her by some invisible agency, and she fell to the floor."

What a spectacle for parents!! But, as the Bible is true, these spirits will "go forth to the kings of the earth and the whole world"!!

CHAPTER II.

REALITY OF SPIRITUAL INTERCOURSE.

THE Bible, profane history, and spiritual manifestations establish the fact beyond all successful controversy, that men have had intercourse with spirits. The advocate of spiritualism is so strongly fortified on this point that before all others he prefers such opponents as deny all agency of spirits in the "manifestations." Against such a position he is best prepared to wage a successful warfare.

In all ages persons have claimed to hold intercourse with spirits, whose claims have never been disproved. It is not to be expected that reflecting and candid persons who believe in the Divine origin of the Scriptures, in the midst of such wonders as surround us, will adopt any theory or philosophical hypothesis to explain these "manifestations," which will not admit of a consistent explanation of all the spiritual phenomena of the Bible, without violence to the plain letter of inspiration—its necromancy and familiar spirits—its Egyptian sorcery and magic—its evocation of Samuel—its pythonric damsel-inspiration of false prophets—its history of possessions by demons and expulsion of demons—its unclean, wandering and seducing spirits—its satanic conversations and satanic miracles—its predictions of "devils working miracles," with its witchcraft and worship of devils. To deny the possible agency of evil spirits in manifestations like these of our times, is to deny the truth of the Bible.

JEHOVAH said to Israel: "When thou art come into the land which the Lord thy God giveth thee, thou shalt not learn to do after the abominations of these nations. There shall not be found among you any one that maketh his son or his daughter to pass through the fire, or that useth divination, or an observer of times, or an enchanter, or a witch, or a charmer, or a consulter with familiar spirits, or a wizard, or a necromancer. For all that do these things are an abomination unto the Lord: and because of these abominations the Lord thy God doth drive them out from before thee."—Deut. 18: 10–12.

I. DIVINATION.—"Divination, the art of foretelling future events by previously recognized signs. The word is derived from the Latin *devinatia*, and that again from *divinus*, forming an acknowledgment of the text—'secret things belong to God!' The Greek word is *manteia*, and this which takes its derivation from *mantis*, a prophet or soothsayer, is generally used in combination to denote the various species of divination. Thus geomancy, necromancy, cheiromancy, from *ge, the earth, nekros, a dead person; cheir, the hand;* and *manteia*, signifying therefore divination by means of sand or earth, by calling up the spirits of the dead, and by investigating the lines on the palm of the hand. Divination appears to have been early reduced to a kind of a system, and we find many prohibitions in the word of God directed against it. . . .The kinds of divination mentioned in Holy Writ, are—

1. Cupellomacy, otherwise Berylomacy, divination by the cup or jewel.
2. Rhabdomacy, divination by the wand or arrow.
3. Necromancy, divination by the dead.
4. Splanchnomancy, divination by inspecting the entrails of victrims.
5. Oneiromancy, divination by dreams.
6. Cleromancy, divination by lot.
7. Idolomancy, divination by teraphim.
8. Phonomancy, divination by voices.

There were some lawful means among the Jews for inquiring into the future. There were the prophets or seers ; there was the Urim and Thummim. God having thus made provision even for the infirmities of the people, all other modes of obtaining a knowledge of future events were forbidden under the severest penalties : to be stoned to death was the punishment denounced against diviners and those who consulted them ; and it is to be observed, that none were likely to do so save those who, on account of the unlawfulness of their designs, could not consult the lawful oracles, or those to whom, on account of their offences, these oracles were sealed. Thus we find Saul declaring to the shade of Samuel : "God is departed from me, and answereth me no more, neither by prophets nor by dreams, therefore

I have called thee."—(1 Sam. 28 : 15.)—*Bible Cyclo. Art. Divination.*

2. Observer of times, one who imputes good or ill fortune to the day when any enterprise is commenced, regarding some days as lucky and other days as unlucky.

3. Enchanter, a person who practices incantation or conjuration ; one who calls up spirits by magic formulas ; one who brings into action the power of spirits.—See Ex. 7 and 8.

4. Witch, a woman who practices divination by the aid of evil spirits ; one who has a divining spirit in her ; one who exerts supernatural power by the aid of a familiar spirit ; "a medium for test personations, by which the actual presence" of evil spirits "can be realized ;" a "developing medium."

"*Witch*, a woman who, by a compact with the devil, practices sorcery, or enchantment."—*Webster.*

5. Charmer, a mesmerizer ; a psychologist ; one who entrances by the assistance of evil spirits.

6. Consulter with familiar spirits, one who consults a spirit that is in him, or by which he is inspired ; one who consults an evil or a departed spirit with which a compact has been made ; one who consults a spirit that inspires another or that is familiar with another.

"*Familiar Spirit*, a dèmon or evil spirit, supposed to attend at call."—*Webster.*

Gesenius defines the original of 1 Sam. 28 : 7—rendered in our version "a woman who hath a familiar spirit"—"*A woman in whom is a divining spirit.*"

"Mediums" of these days say they have divining spirits *in them*. Some say they have made a compact with spirits to be their constant attendants, familiars and guardians. Others say that spirits are obedient to their call. Thus, *Prof. Hare* says, "*spirits do exist obedient to his call.*"

7. WIZARD, a medium for evil spirits, or departed spirits; "a conjurer or enchanter; a sorcerer."—*Webster.*

8. NECROMANCER. Necromancy, Greek *Necromanteia,* is derived from *Nekros,* dead, and *Mantis,* a diviner. It signifies divination or the revealing of secrets by the assistance of the dead.

"*Necromantis,* one who reveals future events by communication with the dead."—*Donnegan—Webster.*

9. SOOTHSAYER, a prognosticator, a foreteller; one who undertakes to tell future events without reliance on Divine inspiration. Balaam, who went to curse Israel, is stylcd a soothsayer.—Joshua 13 : 22.

10. MAGIC, the art or science of putting into action the power of spirits; or the science of producing effect by the aid of departed spirits.—*Webster.*

Jannes and Jambres, who withstood Moses, were styled magicians and sorcerers.

11. SORCERY, magic: with craft; or divination with the assistance of evil spirits.—*Webster.*

In Revelation 21 : 8, sorcerers are classed with murderers, and doomed to perdition.

MR. BRITTAN, Editor of the *Spiritual Telegraph*, expressed his belief to the writer, that the Bible justifies intercourse with spirits ; that only the *idolatrous form* of spiritual intercourse is forbidden. This is a mistake. Our quotation from Deuteronomy prohibits it in six specifications, neither of which involve idolatry. All these, with soothsaying and magic, are comprised in sorcery, which is treated as a heinous crime. " Sorcerers . . . shall have their part in the lake which burneth with fire and brimstone."—Rev. 21 : 8.

Some persons contend that sorcerers, necromancers, and witches, were always mere pretenders, and never had anything to do with spirits. This is incredible. The signs imputed to them, the forms of expression employed, the statements made concerning them, and the severe penalties decreed against their offences, prove the contrary.

1. *The signs* wrought by the magicians in Egypt —such as changing rods to serpents, water to blood, and bringing up frogs into all the land, prove the aid of superhuman power.—See Ex. 7 and 8.

2. *The forms of expression* employed concerning them—" *A consulter with familiar spirits*"—" *A man or a woman that* HATH *a familiar spirit;*" not *pretendeth* to have a familiar spirit. " *The soul that turneth after such as have familiar spirits.*" These passages prove that some persons *really had* fami-

liar spirits, and were not mere pretenders. The Bible exposes pretenders, and would have exposed these if they had been such in this respect ; but it does not contain the least hint of the kind.

Gesenius, the Hebrew Lexicographer, thus defines : Ob, (Plu. Obōth) *nekromantis*, or *nekuomantis*, i. e. a necromancer, sorcerer, conjurer, who professes to call up the dead by means of incantations and magic formulas, in order that they may give responses as to doubtful or future things, specially put (*a*) for the divining spirit, the foreboding demon, python, supposed to be present in the body of such a conjurer. Lev. 20 : 27. *A man or a woman who hath the spirit of divination*, Engl. 'familiar spirit." 1 Sam. 28 : 8. Cōsōmi-nā li bāōb, *divine unto me by the foreboding spirit;* whence such a sorceress is called ēsheth bāălăth ōb, *a woman in whom is a divining spirit*, 1 Sam. 28 : 7, 8.—(*b*) for *the dead, the shade* or *spirit evoked.* Isa. 29 : 4, Vehāyāh kiōb mēēretz kōlèk, *and thy voice shall be like a shade out of the ground.*

Observe, according to Gesenius, Saul's order to his servants literally rendered, was—"*Seek me a woman in whom is a divining spirit.*"—1 Samuel 28 : 7.

"*Baalath-ōb*," says the Bible Cyclopædia, "rendered in our version ' one that hath a familir spirit,' signifies literally 'a mistress of inflation or swelling ;' the pretenders to prophecy, among the heathen, as serted that a spirit of divination entered into them, and caused their persons to swell out to an unusual size. Virgil has described an inflated prophetess of this kind :—

> " The virgin cries the God ! behold the God !
> And straight her visage and her color change,
> Her hair's dishevelled, and her heaving breast
> And laboring heart are swollen with sacred rage.
> Larger she seems, her voice no mortal sound,
> As the inspiring God, nearer and more near,
> Seizes her soul."—*Æneid*, vi.

Virgil's description of the appearance of the prophetess is so analagous to the effect sometimes produced by the spirits on the "mediums" of our times, that no person who has witnessed the entrancement of the latter can fail to discover that the operations are *identical.*

The case of the pythonic damsel of Philippi is in point ;

> " And it came to pass, as we went to prayer, a certain damsel possessed with a spirit of divination met us, which brought her masters much gain by soothsaying. The same followed Paul and us, and cried, saying, These men are the servants of the most high God, which shew unto us the way of salvation. And this did she many days. But Paul, being grieved, turned and said to the spirit, I command thee in the name of Jesus Christ to come out of her. And he came out the same hour. And when her masters saw that the hope of their gains was gone, they caught Paul and Silas, and drew *them* into the marketplace unto the rulers.—*Acts* 16 : 16–18.

Says a writer "we have here an unquestionable proof of such a communication of superhuman knowledge. It may be first observed, that the term used by the sacred writer to describe this woman's occupation, *manteuomai*, and which our translators have rendered 'soothsaying,' signifies 'to *foretell divine, prophesy*, DELIVER AN ORACLE.' It is precisely the same word which is used by Herodotus when referring to the divination of the Scythians, (Lib. 4, cap. 67,) and which is also employed by him when speaking of the famous oracle at Delphi. (Lib. 6, cap. 76 ; *et* lib. 8, cap. 38.) The case is, therefore, strictly in point.

"In this instance, then, it is clear that an evil spirit gave to the woman the power of making superhuman, or *oracular*, communications. The presence and power of this spirit were absolutely necessary to the production of those results ; for, when the demon was expelled, her masters 'saw that the hope of their gains was gone,' and their chagrin and rage led to a fierce persecution."

3. *The severe penalties* decreed against sorcerers, witches and consulters with familiar spirits, and those who possessed them, prove they were not mere pretenders. It is incredible to suppose that Jehovah aimed at a mere pretence, when from the thunders of Sinai he decreed to Israel :

"*Thou shalt not suffer a witch to live !*"—Ex. 22: 18.

"The soul that turneth after such as *have familiar spirits*, and after wizards, to go a whoring after them, I will even set my face against that soul, and will cut him off from among his people. A man also or woman that *hath a familiar spirit, or that is a wizard*, shall surely be put to death: they shall stone them with stones.—Lev. 20: 6, 27.

Now, let those who in the face of such language as this, deny that the offenders here named had intercourse with spirits, take the responsibility of asserting that JEHOVAH *legislated against nonentities!*

"Both the law and the history therefore concede," says Mr. Beecher, "the *reality* of the practice doomed with death, and the reason of the penalty is manifest. Polytheism was the disease to be cauterized. The worship of the dead was the root of Polytheism. Converse with the dead was the root of worship. Odylic arts were the root of converse. Therefore the law struck at the root by prohibiting the whole on the pain of death."—*Beecher's Review*, p. 44.

The New Testament history of Demoniacs proves that spiritual intercourse is real.

"And they came over unto the other side of the sea, into the country of the Gadarenes. And when he was once out of the ship, immediately there met him out of the tombs a man with an unclean spirit, who had his dwelling among the tombs; and no man could bind him, no, not with chains: because that he had been often bound with fetters and chains, and the chains had been plucked asunder by him, and the fetters broken in pieces: neither could any man tame him. And always, night and day, he was in the mountains, and in the tombs, crying, and cutting himself with stones. But when he saw Jesus afar off, he ran and worshiped him, and cried with a loud voice, and said, What have I to do with thee, Jesus, thou Son of the most high God? I adjure thee by God, that thou torment me not. For he said unto him, Come out of the man, thou unclean spirit. And he asked him, What is thy name? And he answered, saying, My name is Legion: for we are many. And he besought him much that he wonld not send them away out of the country. Now there was there nigh unto the mountains a great herd of swine feeding. And all the devils besought him, saying, Send us into the swine, that we may enter into them. And forthwith Jesus gave them leave. And the unclean spirits went out, and entered into the swine: and the herd ran violently down a steep place into the sea, (they were about two thousand;) and were choked in the sea. And they that fed the swine fled, and told *it* in the city, and in the country. And they went out to see what it was that was done. And they come to Jesus, and see him that was possessed with the devil, and had the legion, sitting, and clothed, and in his right mind: and they were afraid. And they that saw *it* told them how it befel to him that was possessed with the devil,* and *also* concerning the swine. And they began to pray him to depart out of their coasts."—Mark 5: 1-17.

"¶ As they went out, behold, they brought to him a dumb man possessed with a devil. And when the devil was cast out, the dumb spake: and the multitude marvelled, saying, It was never so seen in Israel."—Mat. 9: 32.

"And one of the multitude answered and said, Master, I have brought unto thee my son, which hath a dumb spirit; And wheresoever he taketh him, he teareth him: and he foameth, and gnasheth with his teeth, and pineth away: And they brought him unto him: and when he saw him, straightway the spirit tare him; and he fell on the ground, and wallowed foaming. And he asked his

*The original word is *daimon*, or *daimonion*—demon, in all similar cases in the New Testament. These terms are never applied to Satan. He is styled *diabolus*, Beelzebub, ect.

Rev. A. Campbell says: "This evil spirit, whose official titles are the Serpent, the Devil, and Satan, is always found in the singular number in both the Hebrew and Greek Scriptures; while *demon* is found in both numbers, indicating sometimes one, and sometimes a legion."

"In the Scriptures the Greek *daimon* is rendered *devil*, and sometimes, at least, improperly; for nothing is more certain than that different beings are intended by *diabolus* and *daimon*."—*Webster*. *Diabolus* is evidently the *Chief* of "the angels that sinned." Christ alludes to his fall, saying: "He was a murderer from the beginning and *abode not in the truth*."—John 8: 44

father, how long is it ago since this came unto him? And he said, Of a child. And ofttimes it hath cast him into the fire, and into the waters, to destroy him: but if thou canst do any thing, have compassion on us, and help us. Jesus said unto him, If thou canst believe, all things *are* possible to him that believeth. And straightway the father of the child cried out, and said with tears, Lord, I believe; help thou mine unbelief. When Jesus saw that the people came running together, he rebuked the foul spirit, saying unto him, *Thou* dumb and deaf spirit, I charge thee, come out of him, and enter no more into him. And *the spirit* cried, and rent him sore, and came out of him: and he was as one dead; insomuch that many said, He is dead. But Jesus took him by the hand, and lifted him up; and he arose."—Mark 9 : 17–29.

"And God wrought special miracles by the hands of Paul: So that from his body were brought unto the sick handkerchiefs or aprons, and the diseases departed from them, and the evil spirits went out of them. Then certain of the vagabond Jews, exorcists, took upon them to call over them which had evil spirits the name of the Lord Jesus, saying, We adjure you by Jesus whom Paul preacheth. And there were seven sons of *one* Sceva, a Jew, *and* chief of the priests, which did so. And the evil spirit answered and said, Jesus I know, and Paul I know; but who are ye? And the man in whom the evil spirit was leaped on them and overcame them, and prevailed against them, so that they fled out of that house naked and wounded. And this was known to all the Jews and Greeks also dwelling at Ephesus; and fear fell on them all, and the name of the Lord Jesus was magnified. And many that believed came, and confessed, and shewed their deeds. Many of them also which used curious arts brought their books together, and burned them before all *men:* and they counted the price of them, and found *it* fifty thousand *pieces* of silver.* So mightily grew the word of God and prevailed."—Acts 12: 43–45.

Does any one suppose that the so-called spirit possessions were only lunacy? Demoniacs are clearly distinguished from lunatics.

* According to some the Libraries of these sorcerers cost $28,000.

"And his fame went throughout all Syria: and they brought unto him all sick people that were taken with divers *diseases* and torments, and those which were *possessed* with *devils*, and those which were *lunatic*, and those that had the palsy; and he healed them."—Mat. 4: 24.

Some persons contend that these descriptions of possessions by evil spirits, their expulsion and habits are only eastern metaphors. If this were true, it would prove the existence of the spirits, and reality of the possessions, as a shadow proves the existence of a substance, from which it is cast. It would be as difficult to find a metaphor of a metaphor as to find a shadow of a shade.

"On the principle that every demon is an eastern metaphor," says an eminent scholar, "how incomparably more eloquent than Demosthenes or Cicero, was he that had at one time a legion of eastern metaphors within him struggling for utterance! No wonder, then, that the swine herds of Gadara were overwhelmed by the moving eloquence of their herds, as they rushed with such pathos into the deep waters of the dark Galilee!

"I am sure that the Gadarene speculators were cured of their belief in eastern metaphors when they saw their hopes of gain forever buried in the lake of Gennesereth. It requires a degree of gravity bordering on the superlative, to speculate on a hypothesis so singularly fanciful and baseless as that which converts both reason and eloquence, deafness and dumness into one and the same metaphor.

"It is reported by Matthew and Luke, and almost in the same words. 'When the unclean spirit,' says Jesus, 'is gone out of man, he walketh through dry places, seeking rest and finding none. Then he saith, I will return into my house from whence I came out; and when he is come he findeth it empty, swept and garnished. Then he goeth and taketh with himself seven other spirits more wicked than himself, and they enter in and dwell there; and the last state of that man is worse than the first. Even so shall it be also to this wicked generation.' On which observe, that 'unclean spirits' is another name for demons—that is, a metaphor of a metaphor; for if demons are metaphors for diseases, the unclean spirits are metaphors of metaphors, or shadows of shades. Again, the Great Teacher is found not only for once departing from himself, but also from all human teachers of renown, in basing a parable upon a parable, or a shadow upon a shade, in drawing a similitude from a simile. His object was to illustrate the last state of the Jews. This he attempts by the adventures of a demon—first being dispossessed, finding no rest, and returning with others more wicked than himself to the man from whom he was driven. Now if this was all a figure, to illustrate a figure, the Saviour has done that which he never before attempted, inasmuch as his parables are all founded not upon fiction, but upon facts—upon the actual manners and customs, the incidents and usages of society.

"That must be a desperate position to sustain which degrades the Saviour as a teacher below the rank of the most ordinary instructors of any age. The last state of the Jews compared to a metaphor!—compared to a nonentity!—compared to a fiction!"

"When I read of the number of demons in particular persons," says a very distinguished Bible critic, "and see their actions expressly distinguished from those of the man possessed; conversations held by the demons about their disposal after their expulsion; and accounts given how they were actually disposed of; when I find desires and passions ascribed peculiarly to them; and similitudes taken from their manners and customs, it is impossible for me to deny their existence, without admitting that the sacred historians were themselves deceived in regard to them, or intended to deceive their readers."

After many of the Indians of Martha's Vineyard were converted to Christ, they testified that before their conversion they really had intercourse with demons.

At the present day, as Roberts informs us, "the universal opinion in the east is, that devils have the power to enter into and take possession of men, in the same sense as we understand it to have been the case, as described by the sacred writers. I have often seen the poor objects who were believed to be under demonical influence, and certainly, in some instances, I found it no easy matter to account for their conduct on natural principles; I have seen them writhe and tear themselves in the most frantic manner. They burst asunder the cords with which they were bound, and fell on the ground as if dead. At one time they are silent and again most vociferous; they dash with fury among the people, and loudly pronounce their imprecations. But no sooner does the exorsist come forward, than the victim becomes the subject of new emotions; he stares, talks incoherently, sighs and falls on the ground; and in the course of an hour, is as calm as any who are around him. Those men who profess to eject devils, are frightful looking creatures, and are seldom associated with, except in the discharge of their official duties. It is a fact, that they effect to eject the evil spirits by their prince of devils. Females are much more subject to these affections than men, and Friday is the day of all others on which they are most liable to be attacked." *Bible Cyclo. Art. Possession.*

It is no evidence that one is a saint because he casts out devils. Says Christ,

"Many will say to me in that day, Lord, Lord, have we not prophesied in thy name? and in thy name have *cast out devils?* and in thy name *done many wonderful works?*

"And then will I profess unto them, I never knew you: depart from me, ye that work iniquity."—Math. vii: 22.

CHAPTER III.

NECROMANCY IS REAL AND SINFUL.

"There shall not be found among you * * a consulter with familiar spirits, or a wizard, or a necromancer, for all that do these things are an abomination unto the LORD."—Deut. xviii: 11, 12.

NECROMANCY is forbidden by Jehovah, treated in the Scriptures as a reality, and one of the greatest crimes. God has decreed that no man can be just who consults the dead. In consistency and equity he must also have decreed that spirits of the dead cannot be righteous who converse with men. Hence necromancers cannot hold intercourse with departed saints. The spirits of all saints ascend to heaven at death.

"The body without the spirit is dead."—James ii: 26.

"And they stoned Stephen, calling upon *God*, and saying, *Lord Jesus, receive my spirit.*"—Acts vii: 59.

"I am persuaded that he is able to keep that which I have committed unto him against that day."—2 Tim. i: 12.

"Verily I say unto thee, To-day shalt thou be with me in paradise."—Luke xxiii: 43.

"Whilst we are at home in the body we are absent from the Lord. . . We are . . willing rather to be absent from the body and present with the Lord."—2 Cor. v: 6.

"Having a desire to *depart and be with Christ.*"—Phil. i: 23.

When Paul was about to be executed he wrote:

"The time of my *departure* is at hand."—2 Tim. iii: 6.

"Shortly I must put off this tabernacle."—2 Pet. i: 14.

"Then shall the dust return to dust as it was: and the spirit [of the saint] shall return unto God who gave it."—Ecl. xii: 7.

But to the unbelieving Christ said,

"Ye shall die in your sins: whither I go ye cannot come."—John viii: 21.

Now since the departed saints are with Christ in heaven, and sinners are excluded, it is not unreasonable to suppose that the spirits of the wicked are on the earth with their leader, who "goeth about like a roaring lion seeking whom he may devour."

The course pursued by the woman of Endor, proves that she professed to call up the dead. Isa. 8: 19, shows that "familiar spirits" were believed to be spirits of "*the dead*—"

"And when they shall say unto you, Seek unto them that have familiar spirits, and unto wizards that peep and that mutter: should not a people seek unto their God? for the living to the dead?"

The woman of Endor had a familiar spirit which was believed to be a departed spirit, and she professed to be a necromancer. Nothing is said in the Bible to show that these claims were false. So far from it, the language of Isaiah proves that necromancy was a reality, and familiar spirits were spirits of the dead. If this had not been true, the pretence and deception would have been exposed, especially as this very belief and practice was the chief root of all arts of divination and all idolatry.

The fact that Jehovah has made a law with a capital penalty against the discovery of secrets by the assistance of the dead, is sufficient of itself to prove that necromancy was a reality. The penalty is decreed against the *practice*, not against the *pretence;* and the idea that God has forbidden an *impossibility* on pain of death, is too absurd to be tolerated for a moment!

The following argument in proof that the *demons* noticed in the New Testament, were departed spirits, was given by Rev. A. Campbell, in a popular lecture in Nashville, Tenn., March 10, 1841.

"We have from a careful survey of the history of the term *demon*, concluded that the *demons of Paganism, Judaism, and Christianity, were the spirits of dead men.*

1. All the Pagan authors of any note, whose works have survived the wreck of ages, affirm the opinion that demons were the spirits of dead men. From Hesiod down to the more polished Celsus, their historians, poets, and philosophers occasionally express this opinion.

2. The Jewish historians, Josephus and Philo, also avow this conviction. Josephus says, 'Demons are spirits of wicked men who enter into living men and destroy them, unless they are so happy as to meet with speedy relief.'* Philo says 'The souls of dead men are called demons.'

3. The Christian Fathers Justin, Marty, Iræneus, Origen, &c., depose to the same effect. Justin, when arguing for a future state, alleges, 'Those who are seized and tormented by the souls of the dead, whom all call demons, and madmen.†

Lardner, after examining with the most laborious care the works of these, and all the Fathers of the first two centuries, says, 'The notion of demons, or the souls of dead men, having power over living men, was *universally* prevalent among the heathen of those times, and believed by many Christians.'‡

4. The Evangelists and Apostles of Jesus Christ so understood the matter.

As this is very important, and of itself a sufficient pillar on which to rest our edifice, we shall be at more pains to illustrate and enforce it: we shall first state the philological law or canon of criticism, on the generality and truth of which all our dictionaries, grammars, and translations are formed.

Every word not specially explained or defined in a particular sense, by any standard writer of any particular age and country, is to be taken and applied in the current or commonly received signification of that country and age, in which the writer lived and wrote.

* De Bello Jud. cap. viii: 25; cap. vi: sec. 3.

† Jus. Apol., b. i., p. 65, par. 12, p. 54.

‡ Vol. viii., p. 368.

If this canon of translation and of criticism be denied, then we affirm there is no value in dictionaries, nor in the acquisition of ancient languages in which any book was written ; nor is there any confidence to be placed in any translation of any work, sacred or profane ; for they are all made upon the assumption of the truth of this law.

We have, then, only to ask, first, for the current signification of the term *demon* in Judea, at the Christian era ; and, in the second place, Did the inspired writers ever give any special definition to it ? We have already found an answer to the first in the Greeks and Jews of the apostolic age—also, in the preceding and subsequent age. We have heard Josephus, Philo, Lucian, Justin, and Lardner, from whose writings and affirmations we are expressly told what the universal acceptation of the term was in Judea and in those times ; and in the second place the apostles and our Lord, as already said, use this word in various forms seventy-eight times, and on no occasion give any hint of a special, private, or peculiar interpretation of it ; which was not their method when they used a term either not generally understood, or understood in a special sense. Does any one ask the meaning of the word Messiah, prophet, priest, elder, deacon, presbyter, altar, sacrifice, Sabbath, circumcision, &c. ? We refer him to the current signification of these words among the Jews and Greeks of that age. Why then should any one except the term *demon* from the universal law? Are we not, therefore, sustained by the highest and most authoritative decision of that literary tribunal by whose rules and decrees all works, sacred and profane, are translated from the dead to a living tongue? We are, then, fully authorized to say, that the demons of the New Testament were the spirits of dead men.

5. But distinct evidence of the historic kind, and rather as confirmatory of our views than of the authority of inspired authors, I adduce as a separate and independent witness, a very explicit and decisive passage from the epistle to the Smyrneans, written by the celebrated Ignatius, the disciple of the Apostle John. He quotes the words of the Lord to Peter, when Peter supposed he saw a spirit or a ghost. But he quotes him thus, "Handle me and see, for I am not a *daimon asomaton*—a disembodied demon;"—a spirit without a body. This places the matter above all doubt, that with them of that day a demon and a ghost* were equivalent terms.

6. We also deduce an argument from the word

* Our Saxon forefathers, of whom we have no good reason to be ashamed, were wont to call the spirits of men, especially when separated from their bodies, *ghosis*. *Guest* and *ghost*, with them, if not synonymous, were, at least cousins—german. They regarded the body as the *house*, and therefore called the spirit the guest; for guest and ghost are two branches from the same root. William Tyndale, the martyr, of excellent memory, in his version of the New Testament, the prototype of that of King James, very judiciously makes the Holy Spirit of the Old Testament the Holy Ghost of the New; because, in his judgment, it was the promised guest of the Christian temple.

angel. This word is of Biblical origin, and confined to those countries in which that volume is found. It is not found in all the Greek poets, orators, or historians, so far as known to me. Of that rank of beings to whom Jews and Christians have applied this official title, the Pagan nations seem never to have had the first conception. It is, therefore, certain that they could not use the term *demon* as a substitute interchangeable with the word *angel*—as indicative of an intermediate order of intelligent beings above men, and between them and the Divinity. They had neither the name nor the idea of an angel in their mythology. Philo the Jew has, indeed, said that amongst the Jews the word *demon* and the word *angel* were sometimes used in interchangeably; and some have thence inferred that lapsed angels were called demons. But this is not a logical inference: for the Jews called the winds, the pestilence, the lightnings of heaven, &c., *angels*, as indicative of their agency in accomplishing the will of God. In this sense, indeed, a demon might be *officially* called an angel. But in this sense, demon is to angel as the species to the genus: we can call a demon an angel, but we cannot call an angel a demon—just as we can call every man an animal, but we cannot call every animal a man.

But to return to the word *angel.* It is a Bible term, and not being found in all classic, in all mythologic antiquity, could not enter into the Pagan ideas of a demon.* Now, that it is not so used in the Christian Scriptures, is evident for the following reasons ;—

1. Angels were never said to enter into any one.

2. Angels have no affection for bodies of any sort, either as habitations or vehicles of action.

3. Angels have no predilection for tombs and monuments of the dead.

In these three particulars angels and demons stand in full contrast, and are contradistinguished by essentially different characteristics : for—

1. Demons have entered into human bodies and into the bodies of inferior creatures.

2. Demons evince a peculiar affection for human bodies, and seem to desire them both as vehicles of action and as places of habitation.

3. Demons also evince a peculiar fondness for their old mortal tenements ; hence, we so often read of them carrying the possessed into the grave-yards, the tombs, and sepulchres, where, perchance, their old mortalities lay in ruins. From which facts we argue, as well as from the fact that the Pagans had neither Devil, nor angel, nor Satan, in their heads before the Christian times, that when they, or the Christians, or the Jews, spoke of *demons*, they could not mean any intermediate rank of spirits, other than the spirits of dead men. Hence, in no instance in holy

* The meaning of Mr. C. obviously is that the Pagans knew of no angels which were an order of spirits—their angels were only *earthly messengers.*

writ can we find *demon* and *angel* used as convertible terms. Is it not certain then that they are the spirits of dead men?

Statutes, indeed, are ordained and laws promulgated from Mount Sinai in Arabia, from the voice of the Eternal King, against the worship of demons, the consultation of familiar spirits, the practice of necromancy, and all the arts of divination. Hence we affirm that the doctrine of a separate state—of disembodied spirits, or demons—of necromancy and divination, is a thousand years older than Homer or Hesiad, than any Pagan historian, philosopher, or poet whatever.

They make but little argumentative gain who assume that demons are lapsed angels rather than human spirits; for who will not admit that it may be more easy for a demon than an angel who has a spiritual body of his own, to work by the machinery of a human body, and to excite the human passions to any favorite course of action! Were this not the fact, they must have tenanted the human body to little purpose, if a perfect stranger to all its rooms and doors could, on its first introduction, move through them as easily as they.

"If weak thy faith, why choose the harder side?"

7. To this we add the testimony of *James*, who says *the demons believe and tremble* for their doom. Now, all eminent critics concur that the spirits of wicked men are here intended; and need I add

that oft-repeated affirmation of the demoniacs, 'we know thee, Jesus of Nazareth; art thou come to torment us before the time?' Thus all Scriptural allusions to this subject authorize the conclusion that demons are the spirits, and especially wicked and unclean spirits of dead men. A single saying in the Apocalypse makes this most obvious. When Babylon is razed to its foundation, it is said to be made the habitation of demons—of the spirits of its sepulchered inhabitants. From these seven sources of evidence, namely; the Pagan authors, the Jewish historians, the Christian fathers, the four Evangelists, the Epistle of Ignatius, the acceptation of the term *angel* in its contrast with demon, and the internal evidences of the whole New Testament, we conclude that the demons of the New Testament were the spirits of wicked men.

May we not henceforth reason from this point with all assurance as a fixed and fundamental principle?

In one sentence, then, we conclude that there is neither reason nor fact—there is no canon of criticism, no law of interpretation—there is nothing in human experience or observation—there is nothing in all antiquity, sacred or profane, that in our judgment, weighs against the evidence already adduced in the support of the position, that *the demons of Pagans, Jews, and Christians, were the spirits of dead men; and, as such, have taken possession of men's living bodies, and have moved, in-*

fluenced and impelled them to certain courses of action."

Mr. Campbell has presented a conclusive argument. He has shown that when the New Testament was written, the word demon signified the departed spirit of a wicked person. He has shown that Christ and his Apostles never hinted at any other signification nor that that was incorrect. He has given the philological law by which all dictionaries, grammars, and translations are made; and he has authorized the conclusion that we are bound by that law to adopt the signification of the word then in vogue, unless we have positive evidence to the contrary.

It is incredible that he who came to bear witness to the truth, when constantly casting out demons, which his disciples believed were the spirits of the dead, would have neglected to disabuse their minds if they had cherished an error in this particular.

It is no less certain that an inspired Apostle, whose chief antagonists were "wicked spirits," (Eph. 6 : 12, margin,) and who shunned not to declare the whole counsel of God, would have corrected his brethren in this respect, if their belief had been erroneous.

There is no way of fairly avoiding the conclusion that Christ and the Apostles adopted the popular signification of the term *demon* as *the correct one.*

Is it not therefore certain that, at least, some of those demons were spirits of wicked men?

CHAPTER IV.

MODERN PHENOMENA NOT PRODUCED BY HOLY ANGELS.

"And no marvel; for Satan himself is transformed into an angel of light. Therefore *it is* no great thing if his ministers also be transformed as the ministers of righteousness."—2 Cor. xi: 14.

Spiritualists assume that the angels of God are the spirits of deceased persons, and that they are the agents in these manifestations. "Angels," says one, "are the spirits of just men made perfect." "I know of no other angels than the spirits of the dead; all become angels after death," said Mr. Partridge to the writer. We propose to show that this is a mere assumption.

That the celestial angels are neither the agents nor the authors of these developments is obvious from the following considerations.

Angels are a distinct class of beings, widely different in nature and office from these spirits. The latter affirm that they do not eat food like living mortals; and certainly it is difficult to conceive how such diet can be adapted to their natures. But the angels have eaten. When three visited Abraham his servant :

" Took butter and milk and a calf which he had dressed and set it before them, and *they did eat.*"—Gen. 18.

"And there came two angels to Sodom at even; and Lot sat in the gate of Sodom: and Lot seeing *them* rose up to meet them; and he bowed himself with his face toward the ground: And he said, Behold now, my lords, turn in, I pray you, into your servant's house, and tarry all night, and wash your feet, and ye shall rise up early, and go on your ways. And they said, Nay; but we will abide in the street all night. And he pressed upon them greatly; and they turned in unto him, and entered into his house; and he made them a feast, and did bake unleavened bread, *and they did eat.*"—Gen. xix: 1.

These spirits do not pretend to have access to Jehovah's immediate presence. But of the elect angels it was said by the Saviour, "they do always behold the face of my Father who is in heaven."

These spirits are evidently not angels of God in an official sense—that of a messenger from God. They contradict his word, therefore they cannot be sent by him to minister to the heirs of salvation. Professor Hare says : "Spirits of the higher spheres control more or less those below in station, who are sent *by them* to impress mortals." Then they are messengers of demons, not the messengers of God. But the angels of God are "ministers of his, that do his pleasure, hearkening to the voice of his word."* "All . . sent forth to minister for the heirs of salvation."†—They ministered to Abraham,

*Ps. 103: 20, 21. † Heb. 1: 14.

Lot, Elijah, Elisha, Moses, Daniel, Christ, Peter, John and others.

Some portions of Bible truth were communicated to men by the ministry of angels. Jehovah has forbidden all communication with dead men and demons. To contend that Moses received the law at the hand of departed spirits, is to contend that he violated it and incurred its penalty in the very act of receiving it, by practising necromancy, which it strictly prohibits. If departed spirits communicated it they took the most effectual course to exclude themselves from mankind, and to forestall any subsequent revelations which they might choose to make.

While the Bible prohibits all intercourse with the dead, and seeking to those who have familiar spirits, it represents all such as are honored with a visit from an angel of light, as "high favored of the Lord." Hence Paul urges the duty of hospitality to strangers, with the weighty consideration that "thereby some have entertained angels unawares"—referring, doubtless, to the distinguished guests of Abraham, and Lot, in the instances already cited.

Though the angels of God who minister to his people, are constant visitors of earth, their communications have been "few and far between," and contrast strikingly with the hundreds of revelations so cheap and common of the present day, which so forcibly suggest that the residence of the agents, if they are not always walking through dry places and seeking rest and finding none, is to say the least, as far from God the judge of all, the spirits of just men made perfect and the innumerable company of angels as earth is from heaven.

The communications of our times are generally the most trivial and often the most senseless mummeries imaginable. But the angels of God "being greater in might and power," came to men as befits their exalted station, charged with messages of importance, endowed with power to make those messages known and understood to the honor and glory of him they serve.

A marked distinction is made between angels and spirits of the dead, when they are mentioned in connection in the Bible.

Paul makes the distinction when he classifies the inhabitants of the heavenly Jerusalem, as "an innumerable company of angels; the church of the first-born; God the judge of all; and the spirits of just men made perfect."*

The Pharisees made the distinction when they said "If an angel spirit or an angel hath spoken to him."

"The Sadducees say that there is no resurrection, neither angel nor spirit; but the Pharisees confess both."†

This distinction would certainly not have been made, if angels and departed spirits were identical.

* Heb. 12: 22—23.

† Acts 23: 8-9.

The distinction is made by the Saviour. He says:

"Whosoever shall confess me before men, him shall the Son of man also confess before the angels of God: But he that denieth me before men shall be denied before the angels of God."—Luke xii: 8.

Did Christ intend to teach that those who confess him before men should be confessed before themselves? that those who denied him before men should be *denied before themselves?* Who is prepared, in order to sustain a "baseless fabric," to make nonsense of the solemn words of the Redeemer!

Angels are not spirits of the dead, because they existed before any person died.

"Then the Lord answered Job out of the whirlwind, and said, * * where wast thou when I laid the foundations of the earth? declare, if thou hast understanding * * when the morning stars sang together and all the sons of God shouted for joy."—Job 38.

"So he drove out the man: and he placed at the east of the garden of Eden cherubim, and a flaming sword which turneth every way, to keep the way of the tree of life."—Gen. 3: 24.

These *sons of God* and *cherubim* must have been angels. Is it not certain, therefore, that angels existed when the earth was created, and before the death of any person, and consequently are a distinct class of beings?

Let those who assert the contrary in the face of such Biblical testimony, vindicate if they can, the absurdity that the Lord had no angels till after the death of Abel!

CHAPTER V.

SPIRITUALISM NOT THE WORK OF DEPARTED SAINTS.

"Blessed are the dead which die in the Lord from henceforth: yea, saith the spirit, that they may rest from their labors; and their works do follow them."—Rev. xiv. 13.

THE SPIRITS of all departed saints are with Christ in heaven. Those only who have been converted and lived the life of the righteous, together with little children, are eligible to a seat in the presence of the Redeemer, and the holy angels. It is their special privilege to claim what was implied by the dying protomartyr, "Lord Jesus receive my spirit." Well may all such persons "desire to depart and be with Christ; which is far better." Christ's assurance, "Verily I say unto thee To-day shalt thou be with me in paradise," was ample consolation for the dying penitent. Says the Apostle.

"Whilst we are at home in the body, we are absent from the Lord: We are confident, *I say*, and Willing rather to be absent from the body, and to be present with the Lord."—2 Cor. v: 6.

When Christians are absent from the body they are *present with the Lord*. Paul clearly reveals the residence of all departed saints.

"Ye are not come unto the mount that might be touched, and that burned with fire. * * But ye are come unto mount Sion, and unto the city of the living God, the heavenly Jerusalem, and to an innumerable company of angels. To the general assembly and church of the first-born, which are written in heaven, and to God the Judge of all, and to the spirits of just men made perfect, and to Jesus the mediator of the new covenant."—Heb. xii : 18, 22–24.

According to this, in that blessed city, styled the "Father's house of many mansions," are :

1. An innumerable company of angels.

2. The church of the first born, those who rose from the dead with Christ.

3. GOD the judge of all is there.

4. *The spirits of just men made perfect are there.*

5. Jesus, the mediator of the new covenant is there.

As the old Jerusalem was located on mount Sion, by a tropical allusion the location of the new Jerusalem is called mount Sion also. Paul's saying to his brethren "ye are come unto mount Sion," is a metaphor, showing that the relation existing between them and the heavenly city, was analagous to the relation between the Israelites and mount Sinai, when they were at the foot of the mountain and Moses was on its summit, as the mediator of the old covenant; because when Paul wrote, as now, Christ was in the heavenly Jerusalem as mediator of the new covenant.

Does any one suppose that this text describes what is to be realized after the resurrection? I reply, the Apostle speaks of what had already taken place. "Ye are not come unto the mount that might be touched—like Sinai—but ye *have come* unto mount Sion," i. e., they had obtained a relationship of heavenly grace with that city, the *location* of which Paul metaphorically styled mount Sion. And as Paul is true, the abode of departed saints is there.

"We know that, if our earthly house of *this* tabernacle were dissolved, we have a building of God, a house not made with hands, eternal, in the heavens."—5 Cor. v: 1.

It cannot be shown from the Bible that Jehovah has ever commissioned the spirit of a just man to hold intercourse with sinful mortals, with a solitary exception, that of Samuel.

The appearance of Moses and Elias on the Mount of Transfiguration will be urged as an objection to this assertion.

'And after six days, Jesus taketh Peter, James, and John his brother, and bringeth them up into an high mountain apart, and was transfigured before them; and his face did shine as the sun, and his raiment was white as the light. And, behold, there appeared unto them Moses and Elias talking with him."—Math. xvii: 1-4.

Elijah never died. He was translated to heaven bodily.* Hence he must have appeared on the mountain in his glorified body. There was but one disembodied spirit there—that of Moses, and he had no intercourse with the apostles.

Hence this text does not effect our position. His

*2 Kings 2: 11.

holding intercourse with Christ is another matter. The Saviour is not subject to the law which governs sinful mortals. He is LORD of both the dead and the living. It is his prerogative to hold intercourse with both. Many things which were just and possible for him are unlawful and impossible for all others.

Is it objected that the messenger who communicated the Apocalypse to John was one of the prophets who had lived in a previous age?

"And I John saw these things, and heard them. And when I had heard and seen, I fell down to worship before the feet of the *angel* which shewed me these things. Then saith he unto me, See thou do it not; for I am thy fellow-servant, and of thy brethren the prophets, and of them which keep the sayings of this book: worship God."—Rev. xxi: 8, 9.

I admit that this was one of the prophets · but not a disembodied spirit.

There is no hint that it was a disembodied spirit, and it is not necessary to suppose that it was such.

Enoch and Elijah had been translated to heaven bodily. For aught that appears to the contrary, it might have been one of them.

When Christ arose from the tomb—

"The graves were opened; and many bodies of the saints which slept arose, and came out of the graves after his resurrection, and went into the holy city, and appeared unto many."--Math. xxvii: 52.

Paul informs us what became of them subsequently:

"For whom he did foreknow, he also did predestinate to be conformed to the image of his Son, that he might be the firstborn among many brethren. Moreover, whom he did predestinate, them he also called: and whom he called, them he also justified: and whom he justified, them he also glorified."—Rom. viii: 29, 30.

According to this they were glorified—received up into glory. And, as I have already shown, this church of firstborn is in the New Jerusalem, in the presence of God and angels, clothed with incorruptible bodies that "came out of their graves," and are thus distinguished from "the spirits of just men." Says the Rev. J. Litch,

"Christ is the firstborn from the dead, Col. i: 18. If he is firstborn from the dead, he is 'the firstborn among many brethren.' Rom. viii: 29. It is the opinion of some that the general assembly and church of the firstborn are the whole church of Christ.—But the whole church cannot be the firstborn; this is an insuperable objection to that view. To remove the difficulty, it is said, the term 'firstborn' applies to Christ, and that it is his church which is spoken of as the general assembly. To this we reply, the language of the original will not bear that construction. The apostle has not used the definite article *the*, as our translation indicates; and as he should have done had he referred to Christ. But he leaves it quite indefinite. *Panēgurei kai ekklēsia prōtotokōn*, literally translated '*a general assembly and church of firstborn.*' This confines the term *firstborn* to the church; and, as before remarked, cannot mean the whole church, because the whole body cannot be firstborn. The conclusion, therefore, is inevitable, that the 'church of firstborn' is a class of persons born from the dead with Christ, who is emphatically *the* firstborn. But we have already learned from Rom. viii : 29, that he was to be 'firstborn *among* MANY brethren.'— In this event, Christ was the first to rise, and they 'arose and came out of the graves after his resurrection.' That they ever went back again into the grave, or died again is not intimated. 'MANY bodies of the saints which slept arose.' 'That he might be the firstborn among MANY brethren.'— The two accounts agree that *many* were designed, and *many* secured for that purpose."

Now since "*many* bodies of the saints" were raised and glorified, it is by no means reasonable to suppose the messenger to John was a disembodied spirit. No hint is given to that effect, and we are under no obligation to believe that such was the case.

SAMUEL, SAUL, AND THE WOMAN OF ENDOR.

"And when Saul inquired of the Lord, the Lord answered him not, neither by dreams, nor by Urim, nor by prophets. Then said Saul unto his servants, Seek me a woman that hath a familiar spirit, that I may go to her, and inquire of her. And his servants said to him, behold, *there is* a woman that hath a familiar spirit at Endor. And Saul disguised himself, and put on other raiment, and he went, and two men with him, and they came to the woman by night: and he said, I pray thee, divine unto me by the familiar spirit, and bring me him up, whom I shall name unto thee. And the woman said unto him, Behold, thou knowest what Saul hath done, how he hath cut off those that have familiar spirits, and the wizards, out of the land: wherefore then layest thou a snare for my life, to cause me to die? And Saul sware to her

by the Lord, saying *As* the Lord liveth, there shall no punishment happen to thee for this thing. Then said the woman, Whom shall I bring up unto thee? And he said bring me up Samuel. And when the woman saw Samuel, she cried with a loud voice: and the woman spake to Saul, saying, Why hast thou deceived me? for thou *art* Saul. And the king said unto her, Be not afraid: for what sawest thou? And the woman said unto Saul, I saw gods ascending out of the earth. And he said unto her, What form *is* he of? And she said, an old man cometh up; and he *is* covered with a mantle. And Saul perceived that it *was* Samuel, and he stooped with *his* face to the ground, and bowed himself. And Samuel said to Saul, Why hast thou disquieted me, to bring me up? And Saul answered, I am sore distressed; for the Philistines make war against me, and God is departed from me, and answereth me no more, neither by prophets, nor by dreams: therefore I have called thee, that thou mayest make known unto me what I shall do. Then said Samuel, Wherefore then dost thou ask of me, seeing the Lord is departed from thee, and is become thine enemy? And the Lord hath done to him, as he spake by me: for the Lord hath rent the kingdom out of thine hand, and given it to thy neighbor, *even* to David: Because thou obeyedst not the voice of the Lord, nor executedst his fierce wrath upon Amalek, therefore hath the Lord done this thing unto thee this day. Moreover the Lord will also deliver Israel with thee into the hand of the Philistines: and to-morrow *shalt* thou and thy sons *be* with me: the Lord also shall deliver the host of Israel into the hand of the Philistines. * * So Saul died, and his three sons, and his armorbearer, and all his men, that same (following) day together."
—1 Sam. xxviii: 6-19; xxxi: 6.

Here is a well authenticated case of the return from the invisible state of the spirit of a child of God, to converse with a sinful man. We have no sympathy for that principle of interpretation which would "explain away" this plain statement of facts, and make out the whole affair–correct prophecy and all—to have been the result of ventriloquism, jugglery, mesmerism and deception on the part of this woman, and virtually yield the whole Bible to infidels. It would be as proper to believe A. J. Davis and S. B. Brittan when they assert that the history of creation is "*a myth*," and Christianity is "*mythological theology*," as to credit the version of this affair which a few persons desire to palm off on the public. This account is no *myth*, but a plain statement of facts, from which we learn that it was customary then, to practice divination by the aid of familiar spirits—that consulting witches is dangerous business, better adapted to night than day, and fitted for darkness rather than light. Hence Saul chose darkness and a disguise for the infamous work.

Secondly, we learn that witches were sought unto by those whom the Lord had forsaken, and that such as do this are, as a judgment, left to their own delusions, to fill their cup of iniquity. It is written that Saul died for his transgressions, and for asking counsel of one that had a familiar spirit, *to inquire of it*."—1 Chron. x: 13.

Thirdly. It appears that the spirit of a child of God is not adapted to the purposes of necromancy, and unlike the rapping spirits, he has no encouragement to offer for charming or making "mediums;" he engages in no rapping, table-tipping or writing—he makes no effort to subject a person to his control, to rob him of his will, to inspire, or possess his body. Unlike the demons of ancient, and the spirits of modern times, he did not *obtrude* himself into notice, he taught none to seek to him for information. He had no theology to present which does not perfectly accord with the doctrines of the Bible; and he arrogated no prerogatives of Jehovah.

Fourthly. He was in an anomalous work for a saint, was out of his element and "*disquieted.*" His repose was violated. In all of these particulars he presents a striking contrast to the spirits of our times. It is obvious from this account that the *real* appearance of the spirit of a righteous man is an anomaly in necromancy, that when it does occur, it is to the consternation of the "medium" and to announce the doom of her impious employer. *Therefore if the spiritualists have not heard their condemnation from a spirit, it is because they have had no intercourse with departed saints.* If all these spirits teach contrary to the law and testimony it is because they are all from beneath, which is certainly true. This case of Samuel is an isolated one—the only well authenticated exception to an otherwise universal rule. We contend that this was a real appearance of the spirit of a just man, intended to convey an important lesson, and there is no need of another such manifestation. It could never be rendered more effectual in its purposes by a thousand repetitions. There was one Elijah, one Job, one Daniel, one Messiah, one dividing of the sea, one deliverance from a furnace, and one appearance to necromancers of the spirit of a righteous man. While it is granted that by the power of conjuration the spirits of wicked men may be summoned to the presence of mortals, we contend that the abodes of bliss are not subject to the arts of necromancers.

The appearance of Samuel simultaneously with the conjuration, can be reconciled with the principles of God's moral government, only on the ground that the sin and high position of Saul, with the exigencies of the case, rendered that the most effectual moment for Jehovah to strike the decisive blow at necromancy, by *sending* a faithful prophet to doom a rebelious king. *Never was such a rebuke given to the practice of a forbidden art!*

Says Dr. Stilling*—"The enchantress received orders to raise the deceased prophet, Samuel, who, with all the rest of the Old Testament saints, abode in Hades, in a state of blissful rest, until the conqueror of death conducted them in triumph into the mansions prepared for them. The woman employed her art; but instead of one of her familiar spirits, that was to have acted the part of Samuel, he appeared himself, by the divine permission and instigation. This the witch had not expected, she therefore cried out for fear, and said, 'I see Elohim, —something divine! Samuel then announced to

* Theory of Pneumatology by Dr. Johann Jung-Stilling, late Professor of the University of Heidelberg and Marburg, and Private Aulic-Counsellor to the Grand Duke of Baden. Translated from the German by Samuel Jackson, London, 1834, p. 207.

Saul, that the following day he would be with him in the realm of the dead or of spirits."

We are told by Governor Tallmadge and others, that the Apostles John and Paul *have* returned and conversed with men. One writer alleges that they came to explain their writings. If this were true, Paul made a great mistake when he said he had "fought the good fight and *finished* his course." He had no anticipation of fighting his battle over in a disembodied state; much less did he suppose that in this "progressive age" he would become so enlightened as to consider his Christian labors all "loss and dross for the excellency" of spiritualism! His teachings are specially calculated to tare up by the roots the doctrines of spiritualism. The latter denies the resurrection of the dead. But Paul declared that if the dead should not rise at the sounding of the last trump the Christian's hope was vain and the apostles were false witnesses.* If he is now engaged in the same work with these anti-Christian spirits, he must have apostatized, since when living he averred,

> "We wrestle not against flesh and blood, but against principalities, against powers, against the rulers of the darkness of this world, against *wicked spirits* in heavenly places."—Eph. vi: 12.—Margin.

Moreover, he kept very choice company, testifying that "evil communications corrupt good manners,"

* 1 Cor. 15: 13–15, 52.

and that no fellowship should be had with the unfruitful works of darkness.

If the spiritualists are to be credited, Paul and John were very short-sighted prophets. For their writings are specially adapted to forestall any favorable reception which they might otherwise have met, and to counteract any influence which they might have exerted in their spiritual visitations. The former cautioned the world against "seducing spirits and doctrines of demons." The latter referred the doctrines of spiritualism to Anti-christ, and predicted that *demons* should "go forth to the kings of the earth, and the whole world, to gather them to the battle of the great day."

Some persons suppose they have seen the spirits of departed saints, and conversed with them. But the evidences do not warrant this conclusion.

1. It is well known that some persons are at times afflicted by a species of delirium, the result of debility or the derangement of the nervous system. At such times they often see spectres which have no existence except in their disordered imaginations.

A venerable clergyman related to the writer, that once, when on his bed in feeble health, it appeared to him that his bed was standing some distance from its usual place by the wall, and that three men came twice between his bed and the wall and conversed in an undertone. It seemed a *reality* for the time; but as he was satisfied that his bed had not been moved from its usual position, he inferred the whole must have been a mere phantom.

Many saints supposed to have been seen by spiritualists, are, doubtless, the creation of their own excited imaginations.

Dr. Stilling says: "The celebrated Frederick Nicolai, of Berlin, fell once into a state, in which he saw many spiritual beings around him, which all gradually vanished on making use of laxative and cathartic medicines!"

2. Men often psychologize persons and cause them to see whatever they choose to make them see, though the persons appear to be in their natural state, and suppose themselves free from any charm, when in fact they are under an enchantment. Now, since these spirits are generally seen by "seeing mediums"—real clairvoyants, the conclusion is inevitable that the appearance of some spirits to these mediums should be imputed solely to psychological impressions. This the spiritualists will not deny.

3. It is well known that what the mediums term "going into the interior state" is often nothing else than psychologizing themselves. Whatever they may see in that state no reliance can be placed in their visions, all of which should be imputed to a galvanized imagination let loose. They may suppose they see apostles, saints and friends, when none of them are present.

Says Dr. Stilling, in "Pneumatology," p. 72: "I knew a pious female, who, in her trance, was surrounded with angels and conversed with them, too. At length the angels began to sing, the pious soul sang with them, and what was it? A miserable ballad-song, and a common national air!"

4. The spirits are said to mesmerize the mediums. Nelson Selby wrote to the *Telegraph*, under date of June 1, 1855:

"Some two years since, when we were witnessing the manifestations in almost every aspect, we were informed by the spirits (as *we* supposed) that they could magnetize the mediums and excite their phrenological organs. They directed us to place a number of them in a row on seats round the room, after which, by calling on them to magnetize a certain organ, the character of that organ would be simultaneously acted out by all of them. By a request to magnetize the organ it would be instantly done. This was always done without any one touching them. Forming a connection with one of them and exciting some particular organ, would produce the same manifestation in all of them."

Others testify to the same effect. If this is true it follows that the spirits can psychologize their mediums and cause them to see apostles, prophets, saints, or whomsoever they desire them to behold. Messrs. Grimes, Fiske, and others, have often done this. To show how completely under the control of the spirit the medium is in such a case, Professor Grimes, in his "Philosophy of Mesmerism," says: "At Saratoga Spa, in the presence of

Judge Marvin and many other gentlemen, I made a young man, of excellent character, take worthless waste paper for bank notes, and give me a written obligation for a large amount of money which he supposed he had received!"

In view of these facts what reliance can be placed in the visions of any medium? Who can believe that any one has ever seen a departed saint?

5. When Satan prefers to take a matter in hand himself rather than trust his emissaries, he can reveal wonders in a moment of time.

It is written concerning Christ:

"And the devil, taking him up into an high mountain, *shewed unto him all the kingdoms of the world in a moment of time.*—Luke iv: 5.

The devil could produce an impressive picture then. Why may he not do the same now? His reputation must be unmerited if his process of daguereotyping in this "progressive age" is not a vast improvement on that early experiment. It would be very strange if this vigilant deceiver "who deceiveth the whole world," should not apply his skill in presenting pictures of saints and angels. We may be assured he has a hand in this matter.

6. Whatever the agencies are by which modern manifestations are effected, they have the power to present pictures to the natural eyes of those who are not "mediums." Two facts will show this.

In the house of Rev. Dr. Phelps, in Stratford, Conn., "at one time while Anna was in the dining-room, and a cousin of hers and some of the children in the front yard, her attention was arrested by some one entering the front parlor. She went in and saw three gentlemen ; two of them sitting on the sofa, and one on a chair, by the table, all having their hats on, and drawn down over their eyes more than usual ; the one by the table had his feet upon the table, and was reading a paper. She was surprised that neither of them rose up, or looked at her as she entered the room ; and when she was within five or six feet of the one nearest her, he leaned over on one side and fell, chair and all, on the floor, and instantly all disappeared ! She was frightened, and ran to her cousin, who was near the front door. She came in, but no persons were there, neither could they have entered without her seeing them. The chair was thrown down, but no person near who could have done it."—*Modern Spiritualism, p.* 160.

The second case occurred at the house of Mr. William B. Lanning, of Trenton, N. J., on the 8th of February, 1855.

There had been sundry "manifestations" about his office and his house ; but as he and his family had become convinced that all of these spirits were *evil*, and the intercourse was *sinful*, they determined to have nothing to do with then.

On the day above mentioned, the family received what they deemed a solicitation to converse with the spirits. About 11 A. M., Mrs. Lanning, and her six children, between the ages of eighteen and five years, saw on the white wall of a room in the house, the entire alphabet in large, beautiful golden letters, on a dark-bordered tablet. They were placed in six lines, underscored with dark and wide marks. The eldest daughter described the letters as the most beautiful she ever saw. All of the seven persons present saw the tablet distinctly, and conversed about it for some fifteen or twenty minutes, when it vanished from their sight.

It could not have been a reflection from another picture. No cause could be assigned by which it could have been produced, aside from supernatural power. Mr. and Mrs. Lanning are persons of veracity. I heard them relate the fact, and have no reason to doubt it. All parties acquainted with the affair believed it to have been produced by the spirits. Seven persons saw this, and none of them were clairvoyants nor mediums for the spirits.

Now since these emissaries can do these things, would it be at all wonderful if they should undertake to gain influence and accomplish their purposes by presenting the pictures of Apostles and saints? Nay, verily! It would be a greater wonder if they did not.

A man should no more trust his eyes and ears with these spirits and their devotees, than he would trust his confiding and inexperienced son with a thousand dollars, in a den of the most adroit knaves and gamblers.

It is no new thing for wicked spirits to personate saints—for demons to represent themselves as gods.

Tertullian in his Apology for the Christian Religion, challenges all heathendom to a trial of their respective divinities by a Christian ordeal.

Says Tertullian, "Hitherto we have used words; we will now come to a demonstration of the very thing, that your Gentile gods are no one of them greater than another. For a decision of the point, let any one that is judged to be possessed by a devil be brought into an open court before tribunals; when that spirit shall be commanded by a Christian to speak, he shall as truly confess himself a devil there, as elsewhere he falsely claims to be a god; or let one equally be produced who is among you Gentiles judged to be inspired by God, who waits at your altars and is esteemed to be a sacred person by you; yea, though he be actuated by one of your most venerated deities, be it Diana, the heavenly virgin, or Esculapius, who prescribes your medicines, and who pretends to relieve the dying, yet these or any others, when they are summoned, if they dare to lie to the christian summoning, and *if they do not confess themselves to be devils, then let that reproachful Christian's blood be spilt by you upon the spot*"*

From this remarkable challenge of Tertullian, it is obviously no new thing for a demon to prescribe medicine—pretend to relieve the dying—claim to be a god—win a host of obsequious devotees, and

* Tertullian's Apol. chap. 23.

be *in reality a devil!* For such, according to Tertullian, were the renowned Esculapius and Diana, of whom it was said, "all Asia and the world worshipeth."*

To affirm the contrary, and that Tertullian gave such a challenge to the heathen world during the bloody persecutions of Severus without the most ample authority, is to charge him with a fool-hardy recklessness not to be imputed to an eminent Christian teacher. It is certain that unless he was thoroughly fortified in his position he hazarded his life.

Modern spiritualists as readily credit the doctrines of spirits, especially those opposed to Christianity, as the ancients did those of Esculapius, Baal, Nisroch and Diana; while they reject the doctrines of Christ concerning probation, regeneration, the resurrection, future judgment and retribution; and earnestly contend that their "spirits" must be referred to the celestial spheres as all good and orthodox, because some of them prescribe medicines, exhort, and teach "Harmonial Philosophy," while Christ and his doctrines are to be rejected, notwithstanding all the great and good things he ever said and did. But perhaps such a result may be justly imputed to Harmonial Philosophy. Suppose demons do prescribe medicines, repeat some old sermon or exhortation, and even pray? as Mr. Beecher says, "if they have healed more diseases—more than they have generated by con-

* Acts xix: 27.

firmed obsession—it proves no more than the Sisters of Charity prove for Rome."*

As their business is to deceive the world, if they would not do these things when they can gain influence by it, they must be greater fools than knaves.

And who never heard a profane drunkard preach, pray, exhort, prescribe medicines, and even teach Harmonial Philosophy, while under the influence of brandy? As for praying, in the days of Christ they *prayed* that they might not be *tormented* "*before the time!*"

Testimony of the Spirits.

SPIRIT THEOLOGY CONTRADICTED BY SPIRITS.

In 1853, Mr. William B. Lanning, of Trenton, N. J., an esteemed friend of the writer, not being fully satisfied of the real character of these spirits, held the following colloquy with one, through a writing medium. The spirit on being asked if it was right and beneficial for the human race to consult these spirits, replied, "yes, it will make them happier and better." He then testified in substance to the main doctrines of these spirits, and said, though he died an unconverted man he was happy—that departed Christians were among these spirits—all were happy—there was to be no resurrection of the dead, no future punishment, nor day of judgment.

* Essay p. 72.

But on being cross-examined a little, the spirit became very angry and unwilling to answer, and begged to depart—said he would go and get more spirits and return. Said my friend, " No. When you go I want you to stay away ; but at present do you answer my questions. *In the name of the Lord I demand it.*"

The "happy" spirit quailed, and Mr. L. proceeded :

" Is the Bible true ? Yes.

The Bible forbids necromancy and the consulting of familiar spirits. Which shall I believe, you or the Bible ? The Bible.

Why then did you tell me that it was right and useful to consult the spirits ? Because I wanted to deceive you.

What is the business of these spirits with men ? What do you think it is ?

I think it is to deceive. Very well, you are correct.

Are you happy ? No. I am miserable.

Is there a hell ? Yes.

Are you in hell ? No, not yet.

Do you expect to go there ? Yes.

When ? At the day of judgment.

Is there to be a day of judgment ? Yes.

Is there to be a resurrection of the dead ? Yes.

Have you any prospect of happiness ? I HAVE NO HOPE !

In the name of the Lord, is there a good spirit—

the spirit of a departed Christian among all of these rapping and writing spirits? *No, not one.*

Where are the spirits of departed Christians? THE LORD HAS TAKEN THEM.

Why then did you tell my brother in Philadelphia the contrary of all this? Because I wished to deceive him.

Could you deceive him? Yes.

[The brother was a spiritualist.]

Why could you deceive him? Because he is a fool.

Why is he a fool? Because he don't believe the Bible.

Can't you deceive me? No.

Why? Because you believe the Bible.

Will you tell my brother what you have told me? Yes.

I want to hear from you no more; good-bye forever. *Spirit.*—Good-bye forever."

Mr. Lanning is a man of veracity, and this account is perfectly reliable

In the *Supernal Theology*, page 95, the spirits say; "The apostles of Christ have not been at any of the circles formed in this country or on the earth. They are in heaven, except such of them as are appointed to govern the spheres, and they have not descended to superintend circles or write sermons for them."*

The subjoined account, which was published in

* Spirit-Rapping Unveiled, p. 136.

the *Spiritual Telegraph* of Oct. 15, 1853, is said to have been copied from the *John Bull*, an English journal, and purporting to have been a narrative of spirit-intercourse by the Rev. N. L. Godfrey, incumbent of Wertly, Leeds, a clergyman of good repute in the Episcopal Church.

The writer says, on the 4th of July, 1853, he had the following conversation with a spirit:

"Are you one of those seducing spirits spoken of by Paul? Yes.

Are you suffering? Yes.

The spirit of a dead person? Yes.

Have you been in hell? Yes.

Are you one of the angels cast out of heaven? No?

Are you a lost soul? Yes.

Do you go into the earth? Yes.

Do you go back to hell? Yes."

On the 18th of July the following occurred;

"Were you an inhabitant of the world? Yes.

Do you haunt houses? Yes.

Have you ever appeared to any one? No.

Can you appear now? No.

Are you prevented? Yes.

Did you ever read the Bible? Yes.

Do you remember the things you read on earth? Yes.

Do they make you miserable? Yes.

Do you remember the parable of the rich man and Lazarus? Yes.

Have you ever seen the rich man? Yes.

Are you in the same place? Yes.

Can you see Paradise? Yes.

Is there a great gulf fixed between? Yes.

Can they see you? (faintly) Yes.

Are literal fire and brimstone the punishment of hell? Yes.

Are they as dreadful as Jesus Christ has said? Yes.

Are the spirits punished for answering my questions? Yes.

Shall you be punished? Yes.

By whom? Spell the name. Spelled "Devil."

Why do you answer then, are you compelled to? Yes.

By whom? Spell the name. Spelled "God."

Can you resist the power that compels you? No.

Dare you tell me a lie about sacred things? No.

In answer to certain questions, he told us that the spirit is not in, but *about* the table, and retains his human form; he has NO POWER TO MOVE WHEN THE NAME OF JESUS IS MENTIONED. On being asked whether the unclean spirits ever entered into any one, he knocked an affirmative; and when asked 'into whom? and what diseases were caused by their possession?' he spelled 'Madmen,' 'Falling sickness,' (or epilepsy,) 'Palsy,' 'Murder.'

We also learned from him, that there were good angels; that he could see them; that they wander on the earth and protect God's people; but that

THE SPIRITS OF THE PIOUS DEAD DO NOT WANDER, BUT REST." With this latter agrees the Bible:

"And I heard a voice from heaven saying unto me, Write, Blessed are the dead which die in the Lord from henceforth; Yea, saith the Spirit, that they may rest from their labors; and their works do follow them."*

Also to the prophet Daniel, in anticipation of his death, it was said, "thou shalt rest."†

If the spiritualists believe what the spirits say, why not believe these three witnesses? We have their testimony that these spirits are all deceivers; that there are angels—another race of beings; that the saints are at "rest;" that "God has taken them;" that there is not a Christian spirit among all these; that there is a hell; that these spirits must go there; that there is to be a resurrection of the dead, and a future judgment.

One of these also testified, that the man that did not believe the Bible was "a fool," and could be deceived by these evil spirits. Let not the spiritualists congratulate themselves with the idea that no spirits but those who belong to their "low spheres" are deceivers. The ancient idolators had substantially the same theory concerning the spheres which they have, and Diana belonged to the highest sphere, and she succeeded in deceiving and obtaining the worship of "all Asia and the world," and yet, according to Tertullian, if she was summoned to testify in open court by a Christian, she would be constrained to confess that she was a devil!

*Rev. xiv: 13. †Dan. xii: 13.

As God has prohibited necromancy under the highest penalty, and has declared it exceedingly sinful for mortals to hold intercourse with the dead, it follows that if a spirit appears and addresses any person, that fact proves a wish to tempt that person to sin. Such an act shows an utter want of regard to the weal of that person, and none would do thus but a wicked spirit. The appearance therefore of a departed saint is entirely out of the question.

Secondly; To contend that God *permits* the spirits of just men to hold converse with mortals, as the spiritualists maintain, is to declare that a defect exists in His moral government, a defect altogether inconsistent with the character of Him who is infinite in goodness, justice, and mercy. The law that would punish with death the person who takes slow poison, and provides no penalty for, but entirely exculpates the vender, must not only be radically defective in its nature and operations, but be *founded in injustice,* and reflect on the wisdom and goodness of the Lawgiver. Such is not the law by which the universe is governed, and such is not the character of Jehovah.

Since it is wrong and sinful for men to hold converse with departed spirits, *it must be wrong for such spirits to attempt intercourse with men.*

Hence, according to the principles of equity, the appearance and conversation of the spirits of the just, is entirely inadmissable.

CHAPTER V.

CHARACTER OF THE SPIRITS.

"And behold, they cried out, saying, What have we to do with thee, Jesus, thou Son of God? art thou come hither to torment us before the time?"—Matt. viii: 29.

WHETHER these invisible agents are spirits of the dead as they represent themselves, or "angels that sinned," as some believe them to be, their character is obviously evil and deceptive, and all who confide in them will sooner or later pay dearly for their presumption. It is unwise to have any intercourse with them, because *no reliance can be placed in what they say.*

E. W. CAPRON, in *Singular Revelations*, p. 63, writes, "says one you get contradictory answers. This is true; or rather, there are answers obtained in regard to coming events which do not accord with the facts as the time transpires . . . It is a great error that many rush into, who are carried away by a little excitement or wonder, that because there is a medium of communication with spirits, that it is therefore an infallible source of information. There are, undoubtedly, spirits who desire to be noticed, and to answer questions, who are too ignorant to give any instruction, and who would be as likely to tell wrong as right! Swedenborg says there are some 'spirits so ignorant that they do not know but they are the ones called for, when another is meant.' This may be so. We are inclined to think it is, for we have known attempts to be made to imitate the signal which we always get when we call for a friend."

What charitable logic! When spirits imitate the rap of another, it follows that they are ignorant, and think themselves called for! Such conduct is not so interpreted by our laws. On the contrary, when a man counterfeits the signature of another, they punish him as a knave, instead of commiserating him as a fool!

Again, Mr. C. says: "Much depends upon the mind and disposition of persons at the time of asking the questions, for, as all the universe goes by affinities, it needs a pure mind, calm thinker, and deliberate questioner to get communications from spirits of a high order."

From the foregoing quotations we learn—

1. That spirits give incorrect answers and tell lies.

2. Persons who consult them frequently inquire for friends, and are imposed upon by other spirits, who profess to be the ones called for, and who counterfeit their signals.

3. That much depends on the condition of the medium as to the nature of the communications.

Now, since these spirits are so accommodating and pander to the wishes and views of the persons with whom they communicate, and it is uncertain what kind of a communication can be obtained from them, or whether any, what reliance can be placed in them?

S. B. Brittan compares them to Babel worse confounded. He says: "We have never entertained the idea, even for a moment, that all spirits are divine in thought and Godlike in action. . . . Many communications from the spirit world are obviously unworthy of preservation, and the record of them would subserve no important purpose. But the same may be said of much that is uttered by men in the flesh. Let any man make a *verbatim* report of what he hears during a single day, in the street, the market, and the exchange, and he will easily trascend the confusion of Babel."—*Review of Beecher*, p. 74.

What reliable authorities these must be, by whose testimony hundreds are shaping their religious views and indulging a hope of eternal felicity, and whose communications this "Professor" of spiritualism compares to the common low talk of the street and market!

Some of these spirits claim to be those of *dogs, cats and horses*. Mr. Richmond, in his discussion with Brittan, in the *Telegraph*, No. 41, says, "Ahies Cowles, in Austinburg, called up the ghost of a horse—'Old Pomp'—and he *tramped* like a horse on the table."

In another instance "six ladies and gentlemen assembled around a usually sized mahogany table. The spirit of some animal was called for. The raps gave it by the alphabet to be, in the first place, that of a pet dog. Several satisfactory answers were given relative to its name, and that of its late master, the time of its decease, &c. Not fully persuaded that they were dealing with the 'spirit' of a dog, one of the mediums requested that the dog would scratch upon the table, when, to the utter astonishment of all present, scratching, as audible and as loud as ever came from the claw of the canine race, was heard upon the table. This was repeated several times. The next 'spirit' was that of a cat, who revealed the secret that it had been drowned while at a very tender age, in a cistern, by a young lady, who was present. The answers in this instance were correct and satisfactory. After this, a gentleman (who was a medium) asked if the spirit of a favorite horse was present. The raps were in the affirmative. The raps then gave the name of the horse by the alphabet, its ago, the number of years it had been dead, the name of the place where it had been struck by lightning," &c.—*Boston Bee.*

These must have had excellent schools, and made rapid "progress" in the spheres. Whether they were members of the "seventh sphere" we are not advised!

SWEDENBORG says in his larger *Diary*, "when spirits begin to converse with men, put no confidence in what they say, for they will say almost anything, and will *falsify*."

They often contradict each other and themselves; scarcely any two of them bear the same testimony on any subject unless there is some collusion.

Prof. Hare says, "According to the spirits there are seven spheres recognized in the spirit-world."—"The spiritual spheres are estimated as being between sixty and a hundred and twenty miles from the earth's surface."

BACON, through Dr. Dexter, says, "All good and pure spirits therefore do not reside any where near it. Some reside millions of miles distant."*

They gave no less than six contradictory accounts through as many mediums, of the death of the late Czar of Russia.

"Messrs. Editors:—Please do me the favor to publish this: On my arrival in this city, a week since, from France and England, I was surprised to learn that a report was current that I had departed this life some time ago; also that my spirit had rapped out messages, and otherwise manifested itself, some seven or eight mediums in this city, and as many elsewhere having held intercourse with my

* Spiritualism, p. 111.

departed soul. According to one oracle I had fought a duel and got winged ; by another account, I had committed *felo de se,* although it seems that *I'm a "fellow" yet, d'ye see.* One said I died in Germany; another in France ; and still another, between Dover and Dieppe, France or England.—But, sir, to quote from Webster, *non verbatim,* 'I ain't dead yet.'—PASCHAL RANDOLPH.*

A. Cridge, a votary, says some of the spirits are "narrow-minded," "debased," "selfish," and "deceptive." †

They said, last summer, that Dr. Kane and his party of the Arctic expedition were dead ! but they have now returned to prove the spirits false.

Mr. Sunderland, of Boston, was a very enthusiastic spiritualist, and devoted a journal to its advocacy for a time ; but the continuation of his *Spiritual Philosopher* was superseded and his ardor completely cooled by the following thorough illustration of the system.

A writer in the *New York Express,* who styled himself Shadrach Barnes, in Feb. 1851, prepared an ingenious ordeal, and fairly caught Mr. Sunderland in a trap, by writing a letter, of which the following is a correct copy :

"respected sur I send one dollar if you please ut have some questions respecting of my daughter which departed this lif january the 19, 1851 i brot

* S. Telegraph, No. 178. † Epitome of Spirit Intercourse, p. 77.

her up from a child she was a daughter too me her name is mary ellen Perkins, and was 19 when she dide my mind is exercised very much in respect of her state of mind in a religious point of view which if you communion with Spirits in the other world she was flitey and out of her head as the poet says afflictions soar long time she bore physician was in vain send me a letter i want to hear if her state of mind is happy no more at present. PHEBE NEWELL

"new Yorc sity Feb the 31st 1851.

"mr laroy Sunderland"

Shadrach enclosed a dollar in this letter to pay Mr. Sunderland for the information desired, and in due time received the following reply.

"ELLIOT-STREET, BOSTON, MASS.

"Half-past ten o'clock, A. M., Feb. 15, 1851.

"My Sister Dear: I have this moment laid your letter before the spirits, and received the following answer: 'Tell her Mary is happy, and with her dear mother Newell all the time. I watch over her for good; and I love her now more than ever.

"I will be near her, and stand by her when she reads your answer. She must not grieve. I will soon make sounds in her presence when she is alone, which she can hear, when she will know it is me!

"And I understood the spirits to say that you are not her own mother, but she loved you as her own, and she said she came here to tell what to say to you when I answered your letter.

" In the sphere where Mary has gone none are miserable, but all are happy as they can be.

" Yours truly,

" La Roy Sunderland.

" P. S. It is not often that I attempt an answer to letters like yours, but I suppose I was attracted to Mary's sweet spirit to gratify you. She has stood by me while writing, as I believe.

" L. S."

Mr. Sunderland kept the dollar as the reward of divination, and the important information received from the spirits.

He learned in due time, however, that the sorcerer had been hoaxed, that "Phebe" was a fictitious character, and " Mary's sweet spirit," was a Delilah. The press heralded the story through the land, spirit communications became a laughing-stock, as they deserved, and Mr. Sunderland was completely cured of sorcery.

Mr. Partridge, of the *Telegraph*, informed the writer that the greatest obstacle to the progress of spiritualism was the implicit confidence which many persons religiously inclined were wont to repose in all the spirits say.

A virtual acknowledgment of what ought to be universally understood, that the spirits are deceivers, and that honest and confiding people are not fit for sorcerers, nor to hold intercourse with their divinities.

The most ingenious of these spirits, those who

make the greatest pretentions to sanctity, are unable to disguise their vile purposes. Any living man who would attempt to teach, and make such silly, contradictory, deistical, and false statements as these, who represent themselves to be prophets, Apostles, and even the Messiah himself, would be a laughing-stock and deemed a fit subject for the Insane Asylum.

They deny the Divine authenticity of the Bible, and degrade its prophets and Apostles to a level with "mediums" and sorcerers, and make them out to have been liars and impostors of the worst stamp, in pretending to have been inspired by the Holy Spirit when writing the book.

The "*spirits*" *through R. P. Ambler*, teacher, p. 46, speaking of the Bible: "The seers and prophets whose names are mentioned in the primitive history, were mediums. * * It was in this manner that the writings of the Bible, which have been properly termed the Scriptures, were originated. * * Therefore will the spirits assure the world that the Bible is not the direct and infallible word of God. * * The *spirits* would claim the authorship of these records as they were primarily given to the world."

A spirit representing himself to be St. Paul, through MR. HOAR, medium, says, "The Bible, when first written, was nothing more than a book written through mediums, as I am now writing through my medium. Its contents were not composed of all the books that are in it at present. Some of the Old Testament was written by men who had no more power than I had to preach the gospel before my conversion." He goes through the Bible thus ;

GENESIS.—" About as true as any fictitious work that is now in print," p. 10.

EXODUS.—" As good a book as could be expected in that day," p. 10.

LEVITICUS.—" Not directly from God, as man supposes," p. 12.

NUMBERS.—" Such an absurdity as that [the facts stated in chap. 1st] ought to be cast into the lowest depth of the infernal regions," p. 13.

JOSHUA.—" Almost the whole book is false," *Ib.*

JUDGES.—" About the same as the others ; and it needs no argument to show that it is void of inspiration," p. 14.

RUTH.—" Without inspiration, the same as the others," p. 15.

SAMUEL.—" A part of it is correct," p. 15.

KINGS.—Multitudes of mistakes—not correct—no inspiration," pp. 16, 17.

EZRA.—" By a person bearing its name, without inspiration," p. 17.

JOB.—" Written through mediums—would have been correct, had it not been that men destroyed its purity," pp. 18, 19.

PSALMS.—" Written in the same way and some of them correct," p. 19.

The rest of the books of the Old Testament are said to be "somewhat correct in the main," p. 20.

"Let me say unto you, O man! at this day, in regard to the Old Testament, 'MENE, MENE, TEKEL, UPHARSIN," p. 21.

In passing through the Gospels, Epistles, and the Apocalypse, this vile spirit exclaims, "Not correct," "mistake," "fictitious," "contrary to the will of God." And to cap the whole, "Such, O man, are the principles the books you call the Bible, are conveying to the inhabitants of the earth. O horrible!" p. 92.

"The Old Testament, which Christ declared wrong and wicked, you are still calling the Word of God. . . . Although your angelic fathers, by the wisdom of God, are allowed to come unto you, and do away with the wicked precepts of your Bible," pp. 93, 94.*

The language of this impostor presents a striking contrast to that of the real Apostle:

"All Scripture *is* given by inspiration of God, and *is* profitable for doctrine, for reproof, for correction, for instruction in righteousness: . . That the man of God may be perfect, thoroughly furnished unto all good works."—2 Tim. 3: 16, 17.

"Though we, or any angel from heaven preach any other gospel unto you, than that ye have received, let him be accursed."—Gal. i: 9.

A FALSE CHRIST.

"There shall arise false Christs."—MAT. xxiv: 24.

A spirit, in 1852, revealed himself through M. L.

* Spirit Rapping Unveiled, pp. 91, 92.

Arnold, of Poughkeepsie, N. Y., as "GOD'S HIGH AND HOLY SPIRIT JESUS CHRIST, FORMERLY OF NAZARETH!"

This false Christ has communicated several volumes. To show his real character we quote from one, entitled "The History of the origin of All Things." It seems Mr. Arnold secured the copyright of a revelation which he supposed he had received direct from the Saviour of the world! His genius says:

"Adam existed about 6,000 years before the deluge," p. 27.

"Noah's death was 600 years after the flood," p. 33.

[This would make Noah 1,200 years old at his death!]

"Freewill is man's Deity," p. 22.

"My medium first acted in his own will. . . Then I commenced trying him with doubts and false impressions, by *fooling* him, as he called it," p. 36.

"I help this medium on all occasions, either apparently trifling, or even *immoral*," p. 50.

"I am and will be the comforter of all who receive me as an emanation from God's Son, or Sent, or as Christ, or as the Holy Spirit. I am not particular about names, p. 63. At last every spirit will be equally the son of God, p. 49. The first thing I call on you for is your heart. Unless you give me your heart you cannot *do me any good*, nor advance your own salvation, p. 70. The parent stock of Noah . . . never secured permanent sway beyond their original boundaries. The last time their sway extended over Asia was ten thousand years ago, p. 41."

"I called myself John, in the beginning of this chapter, not because that was my name in the body, but, because my servant John acted for me in writing the book of Revelation, and united with me in explaining now, what then he did not fully understand. Besides, he is a high son of God, being in the sixth circle of the sixth sphere. He is a noble spirit, who delights to serve God, and who did reveal himself to my clairvoyant spirit, Davis, when he was submissive to his directions," p. 62.

"The Man of the Antediluvian world was a very different being from the present Man. He was larger, stronger and more sensual. He was also six fingered and six toed, and bull-necked. He had a tail; and, it was the apparition of beings of the antediluvian birth, that caused the popular notion of the appearance of evil spirits with tails. He also had horns, short and strait, proceeding from his forehead, p. 97."

"Did Joshua march his men about Jericho for seven days, till the walls fell at the sound of the trumpets? Yes. But meanwhile his armies had underworked the walls, and his attentive enemy had only watched his outward manœuvres. Did the sun and moon stand still at his command or prayer, so that the daylight and moonlight were prolonged? Yes. The sun and the moon were upon the banners of the Cananites; and by his prayer to God, they were brought to a standstill upon Gibeon, and Ajalon. Then the light of day was prolonged by a peculiar kind of zodiacal light, sometimes seen in those regions."—p. 44.

"This Book . . . has been written . . . by the direct revelation of the Son of God, Jesus Christ, formerly of Nazareth."—p. 5.

"When Jesus started for Bethany, he did so by a Divine intimation that Lazarus was sick . . . His sisters tried to persuade Jesus, that their brother was already corrupted, by decomposition of the body having commenced. Jesus knew better than they did, for he perceived he had been buried in a trance . . . His life was *saved*, not restored. He was not dead but was in a trance . . . To all appearance, the dead was raised. But yet there was no such violation of God's order, and law."—p. 45.

"*Were it necessary, I would confirm the truth of this revelation by miracles: such as raising the dead or healing the sick. But the time has not yet come for these. When the time comes it shall be done;* [i. e. when the spirits have subjected a plenty of victims to diseases, such as blindness, palsy, and epilepsy, and have sufficiently practised the art of suspending and restoring animation to attempt to imitate a resurrection without too much risk,] *and through this medium first.*"—p. 75.

What a murdering of chronology, history, and

theology! And yet this book is one of the best and most consistent which the spirits have produced on a similar subject, and this vile personator of the Messiah is a superior representative of this whole race of spirits. If they appear thus in disguise, what must they be unmasked!

Lying Wonders.

"AFTER THE WORKING OF SATAN WITH LYING WONDERS."—2 THES. II: 9.

The following account of prediction and cure, will serve to illustrate the mode of procedure sometimes adopted by the spirits:

"Mrs. Capron and Mrs. Tamlin were in Mr. Tamlin's house alone, when a rapping commenced and gave the signal for the alphabet. On repeating it over, the following sentence was spelled out: 'Sarah (Mrs. Tamlin), *is going to be sick.*' As she was then apparently as well as usual they were somewhat surprised, and Mrs. Tamlin said: 'why! not very sick am I?" The answer was 'yes, very sick, and Rebecca had better not stay alone with you this afternoon." This was some time in the forenoon. Mrs. C. went home at noon and returned about one o'clock and found Mrs. Tamlin vomiting severely. She soon fainted, and continued to have fainting fits of very long duration all the afternoon and through the night. Every time she was about to faint we were told by the sound, which would sometimes spell out "*watch her.*" The same faithful guardian told us what medicine to administer—what to do—told when it would be safe for a part of the watchers to leave—(told them two hours before the time of leaving)—just how many fits she would have during the night—when she would begin to recover, and when she would be well—and all was fulfilled to the letter."—*Singular Rev., p.* 60.

It would be difficult to avoid the conclusion that in this instance as in others, a demon performed the part of prophet, tormentor and physician. They often produced the most violent fits in the days of Christ, and it is no uncommon feat of theirs at the present day. We shall be much surprised if they do not suspend the animation of some obsequious dupe for a short time, in order to gain the reputation of raising the dead. In this particular case, the spirit played a part not unlike that performed by Smith, the Mormon prophet. It is related of him that, cherishing a bitter animosity against Governor Boggs, for driving him and his followers out of Missouri, he made a public prediction that the governor would die before the expiration of a year. Anxious to be a true prophet, he early dispatched his most efficient protege with rifle in hand, to shoot the governor. The vigilant emissary was missed from Nauvoo, when one of the faithful thus interrogated the prophet: "Brother Joseph, where has Rockwell gone? The Prophet replied, "*O! he has gone to fulfill prophecies!*"

About that time a bullet passed through a pane of glass, and made a very sensible impression on the back of the Governor's head, and thence glanced into his neck; but from the effect of which he speedily recovered, to prove Smith a *false* prophet, while Rockwell went unhung to be shot in Nauvoo, by "a gentile."

But the spirit who made Mrs. Tamlin sick was

subject to no such contingency. He did not do his business by proxy. He could fulfill his own prophecies. He could foretell that Mrs. Tamlin would be sick—how sick he intended to make her, and just how many fits she would have! And as he knew when he intended to strangle her, he would kindly tell her friends to "watch her!" "The same faithful guardian told when it would be safe for a part of the watchers to leave—just how many fits she would have during the night, and when she would recover! And all of this two hours beforehand. Wonderful!

It is nothing new nor uncommon for demons to utter prophecies on the strength of a purpose to fulfill them. Augustine says, "they for the most part foretell what they are about to perform."*

A spirit through M. L. Arnold, medium, says of him—"He shall go forth with power to perform miracles, and to make outward signs, even as I may direct him, to reveal their coming or *intended performances*."†

Judge Edmonds understands their predictions to be generally mere declarations of what they intend to perform. He says, "for instance they say on such a day a thing will happen. By this they mean that they *will do the thing*."‡

Some years since they foretold that an infant brother of Almira Bezely, a medium in Provi-

* Beecher's Essay, p. 47, from Kiel Opuscula Academica, ch. iii.
† Hist. of All Things, p. 110. ‡ Spiritualism, p. 455.

dence, R. I., would die at a specified time, and then instigated her to fulfill the prediction by poisoning him!

The foregoing is not the only instance in which demons have wrought "lying wonders." Doubtless nine-tenths of all their pretended cures are of the same character. For the sake of fairly representing their claims to the public, we insert a few more of a similar character—those which Mr. Brittan adduced in his Review of Beecher, to prove the benefit of spiritualism. He admits that he "selected some of the most favorable specimens of spiritual facts." He says, "we insist that the real character of the spirits is most clearly revealed in what they do and say." Let us consider some of these "most favorablo specimens."

"Rev. H. H. HUNT, relates that while in Indiana, in September, 1851, a child, a son of D. C. Smith, was very sick. The physician having given the most favorable medicines for stopping the fits, without effect, the father called me in. I seated myself by the boy, and was put in communication with him by an unseen agency. Soon the patient showed too clearly that another fit was coming on; but instead of his suffering from the attack, *the whole power of the malady fell on me.* The agonizing distress, the clenched fist, and contracted muscle gave me alarm for my own safety; but the second thought that I was in the hands of Spirits, quieted me; and I threw off the attack. *The boy had no more fits, but got well.*"*

It is obvious that the spirits caused these fits; and they had only to suspend operations and

* Review of Beecher, p. 67.

leave the boy in order to deceive their followers with the idea that they had performed a miracle! Mr. Hunt says, "*The whole power of the malady fell on me.* The agonizing distress, the clenched fist, and contracted muscle, gave me alarm for my own safety; but the second thought, that *I was in the hands of the spirits* quieted me." Mr. Hunt was conscious that he was "in the hands of the spirits"—that they had left the boy, and were now attacking him.

If Mr. Hunt is to be believed, the *tormentors* performed the cure. Yet, probably, not only Messrs. Hunt, Brittan, and Partridge, but the whole class of spiritualists, swallow this as a *wonderful miracle!*

Again, says Mr. Brittan:

"The following instance of a remarkable cure by the aid of spirits, is related by Mr. John O. Wattles, a gentleman of intelligence and veracity:

"My brother-in-law related to me an incident that may be interesting to some. A few days before I was there, he was at work in the grove, chopping wood; a young man rode up and inquired 'if his name was Whinery?' He said, 'Yes.' 'Well, you are the man for me; my sister has been at the point of death more than six hours, and the spirits say, 'You can cure her.' Whinery said, 'I can't do any thing; I never did anything in my life—I do not know anything about it.' But the young man insisted, and he went—it was nine or ten miles. When he got there he found a house full of people in attendance, expecting every moment that the young woman would breathe her last, and anxiously awaiting his arrival. When he entered the room, he saw the young woman lying in great agony, the blood frothing from her mouth—in a fit, I suppose. At this sight he sickened—as he does at the sight of blood—and fell back into a chair. He then became entranced, and said, '*In twenty minutes I will lay my hand on her head and she will recover.*' He commenced jerking severely—as was related to him afterward—and immediately the young woman was relieved! At the expiration of twenty minutes he aroused, and turning to the young woman, asked her how she felt—at the same time laying his hand on her head. She answered, '*I am well'—and immediately sat up in bed!* He then went out to supper, and after that returned to the room, and the young woman was up and clothed, and in her right mind. She had been in a partially deranged condition more than a week. She now walked about the room with him, and was standing in the door when the physician—who had left her a short time before, and had come back, not expecting to see her alive—rode up. Being a disbeliever in all the late 'manifestations,' he looked astonished—gazed at her a moment, as if disbelieving his own senses, and exclaimed, 'Gods! No more use for doctors!' and rode off. This can be attested by more than forty persons."*

This was a very clever feat for the spirits. Doubtless their success surpassed their expectations. It seems they had possessed a woman and made her crazy for more than a week, when, the restless tormentors, anxious for another victim, sent for a man whom they could paralyze by the sight of blood—he came—they *strangled her, and caused spasms and "great agony, the blood frothing from her mouth!"* At this sight the man fainted, when they left her and took possession of him before he recovered. He was astonished to find himself a medium; and she ex-

* Review of Beecher, p. 67.

claimed "I am well!" Thus the spirits killed two birds with one stone. They gained another victim, and the honor of performing a miraculous cure. We are "specially impressed" to say, that a cure similar to that which a man effects by relaxing his grasp on the throat of another, whom he had choked till he caused "great agony, the blood frothing from his mouth," *must* be "remarkable!" *Perhaps* there would be "no more use for doctors" while he was living, especially if no other diseases existed but those of his own production. At least a practitioner of no other school could successfully compete with such a sanguinary Titan.

If in the progress of sorcery it should be learned that a man becomes a *superior* physician by virtue of such performances, doubtless nine-tenths of this class of "lying wonders" of the spirits will be deemed "remarkable cures!" None but spiritualists can make such discoveries nor appreciate such doctors.

The duplicity of the spirits is only equalled by the credulity of their dupes, who are trumpeting forth such operations as miracles, and glorying in their own shame.

Rev. H. H. Hunt, of Indiana, relates the following wonder:

"At a circle held at Adrian the first Saturday in July, the spirits wrote: 'Seek the lame, the halt, and the infirm, and they shall be healed.' I then remarked to J. M. Reynolds: 'It can not be done; if that is read, away go the spirits and the cause together; for some one will be presented and not cured.' Nevertheless, the call was read by my colleague, when Mr. Lyons presented himself, stating that *his leg had been drawn up by rheumatism four years, and was under acute pain at the time.* Without the exercise of my own volition, I was thrown into the spiritual state, and placed before him. I was also made to speak by the power of the spirit. * * * * *I put my hand on him, and he was made whole. He dropped his cane and went away rejoicing, fleet as a boy of sixteen.*"*

In this case as in all the foregoing, the demons were only undoing their own work. They had contracted the muscles four years previous, and when the fortunate moment arrived to turn a feat to good account, they caused "acute pain"—gave his leg an electric shock which relaxed the affected part, and then left their victim.

Nor should this version of the affair be deemed incredible by the spiritualists. They should be the last persons to talk of incredibilities. They say the spirits are swayed by passions and caprice, like living men. The rulers of France kept an unfortunate victim in the doleful Bastile forty-seven years. Is it strange that an evil spirit causes a disease of four years?

A more remarkable case occurred in the days of Christ:

"And behold there was a woman which had a spirit of infirmity eighteen years, and was bound together, and could in no wise lift up herself."

* Review of Beecher, p. 69.

In this case it seems a *spirit* had caused an infirmity *for eighteen years!* Christ immediately healed her, saying :

"And ought not this woman, being a daughter of Abraham, whom SATAN *hath bound these eighteen years*, be loosed from this bond on the Sabbath day?"—Luke xiii: 11-16.

This presents the philosophy of spirit-cures. The diseases are caused by the spirits themselves.

"Satan . . . smote Job with sore boils from the sole of his foot to his crown."—Job ii: 7.

Christ "was casting out a devil, and it was *dumb*. And it came to pass, when the devil was gone out, the *dumb spake;* and the people wondered."—Luke xi: 14.

The spiritualists boast that most of the diseases which the spirits have cured are those which have baffled the most skilfull physicians. This is because the victims are either demoniacs, or in some way afflicted by these emissaries of Satan. When the Great Physician was on the earth "he went about doing good, and healing all that were oppressed of the devil."*

These spirits are endeavoring to gain influence by counterfeiting the miracles of the Redeemer.

There are probably not less than two thousand persons in the United States, in various ways afflicted and subjected to their discipline for the purpose of deceiving the public with counterfeit cures whenever they can be turned to account for spiri-

* Acts x: 28.

tualism. They cause the above mentioned diseases, blindness, all the various manifestations of demon-possession, besides I know not how many others.

Theophilus Savill, a young Englishman, stated to the writer, that in April last he was *struck blind* by the spirits nine times in five days, and once he continued so for two hours.

He said, that he told his father he was going to Australia; that his father was a "medium," and replied, "I say thou shalt not go, and thou canst not go." The son declared the spirits could have no power over him. The father conjured the spirits, and they closed the young man's eyes so that it was impossible for him to open them.

Doubtless they will attempt to counterfeit every miracle performed by the Saviour, not excepting the opening the eyes of the blind and the resurrection of the dead. They have declared their purpose to raise the dead, and selected two mediums to be honored by an agency in the performance.

Thus when Mr. Spear of Boston pronounced his inspired benediction on Mrs. Mettler of Hartford, he says, "*Thou shalt say to the dead Arise! and it shall come to pass!*"*

A spirit, in 1852, through M. L. Arnold of Poughkeepsie, N. Y., says, "I would confirm the truth of this revelation by miracles, such as *raising the dead*, and healing the sick, but the time is not yet come

* Fowler's Essay.

for these. [They had not the subjects disciplined for the performances then.] When the time arrives it will be done."*

So it seems Mrs. Mettler and Mr. Arnold are chosen for this sublime work.

Now *if* these spirits are not liars, they will certainly raise the dead!—though the one which inspired Mr. Arnold, declares such a thing to be a "violation of God's order and law"!† The process by which they will probably attempt to imitate a resurrection, will be that of suspending and restoring animation, as illustrated by the following letter by Nelson Selby of Maynon, Illinois, published in the *Telegraph* of June 1, 1855.

"We had been informed that there was a pole of death situated somewhere, but no one knew where. We asked the spirits to inform us where it was situated, which they did by causing one of the medium's hands to be placed (I think) under the right shoulder-blade. When any one formed the connection with one of them, and touched that spot, the manifestation would appear in all. I have, in a great number of cases, called and seen others call, on the spirits to excite the pole of death in three or four or a dozen mediums, when they would immediately begin to draw their breaths as a dying person naturally would; and in a few moments they would close their eyes and fall to the floor, when it would not be in the power of physicians or any one else to detect the least signs of life in them. Nor was it in our power by manifestations or any other means to bring them out of that condition. After our curiosity was sufficiently gratified, we would request them to demagnetize the organ, when the first symptom of returning life would be

* Hist. of All Things, p. 75. Ib., p. 45.

a feeble pulse. We discovered that the oftener they were thrown into that condition the harder it seemed to bring them out, which alarmed us, and we desisted from the experiment. As they would begin to come to, they would express a desire to remain in that condition, as it was delightful."

The foregoing *cures!* said to have been performed by the spirits, have been several times presented as the strongest arguments for spiritualism. When the real facts are understood, but little credit is due for their performances. There was no ejecting or casting out spirits ; they had it all in their own way, and performed for the interests of their own cause. Doubtless they will be ever ready to leave one medium temporarily, in order to gain another.

Malevolence of the Spirits.

They destroyed not less than two hundred dollars worth of furniture in the house of Dr. Phelps, of Stratford, Conn., and not less than twenty dollars worth of clothing belonging to the family, all "for fun," as they declared. By the use of matches they set fire to some papers in the doctor's Secretary, and before it was discovered a score of valuable letters and papers were destroyed. At the same time papers were set on fire in two closets under the stairs.

A lad connected with the family seemed to be the special victim of their malice. He suffered much in various ways. His clothes which he wore were often badly torn ; he felt sensations as though he was pinched, and pins were sticking in him; stones were often thrown at him, and also at others of the family.

A daughter of Mr. Phelps, in anticipation of a pleasant visit to New Haven, had attired herself in a valuable dress, and was standing on the piazza near the front door, the chamber window being open, when a quantity of ink was thrown out of the window by the spirits in such a manner as to totally ruin the dress. Says Mr. Capron, "I cannot conceive of any feelings short of shear malevolence that would prompt such an act."

The reason given by the spirits for thus haunting the house of Dr. Phelps, was that murders had been committed in the vicinity. Very significant! —The regions of crime are not congenial to the righteous.

A prominent spiritualist assigned to the writer as a reason why the spirits annoyed Mr. Phelps: "He was one of these superstitious men who think they must pray to God every day, and they wanted to tease him and teach him better!"

Christianity has nothing to hope from such a source.

It is said they often delight in mischievous pranks, such as teasing their mediums by disclosing their secrets in the presence of others.

A young lady in Providence, R. I., a medium who had been much injured by mesmerism and spirit mediation, was tormented day and night for a long time by constant knocks and raps. Unable to obtain any quiet repose or refreshing sleep, her life was a continued scene of suffering and sorrow. Nothing short of malignity could have instigated such tormentors.

The Spirits are Demons.

Nothing is more certain than that these spirits produce the same phenomena, and hence belong to the same class with the demons—Greek *daimōnia*—which anciently were deified by the heathen nations, inspired soothsayers, spoke in oracles, controlled omens, lurked in images, haunted the abodes and possessed the bodies of men and of beasts. The spiritualists testify that this is true, and that a large share of the modern phenomena correspond to the lowest phases of the ancient manifestations.

Mr. Newton, of the *New Era*, says "the Rev. Charles Beecher, 'concludes that the movement is essentially one with the *demonic* possession whereof the Gospels often speak—that is, the control and use of the bodily organs of the living, by human spirits, *incorrectly termed 'devils'* in our English version of the Scriptures.' This position, remarkable as it is, is unquestionably correct as regards a great portion of the manifestations which have been made in various parts of the country."*

Now since these spirits are the same with the demons of ancient notoriety, it is only necessary to

* Letter to the Edward's Church, p. 16.

ascertain the character of those, and in what light they were regarded by Christ, the Apostles and early Christians, in order to decide the character of these, and our duty concerning them.

The origin of the word *daimōn* is lost. Dr. WEBSTER, with all his facilities for extensive research, says: "The origin and primary sense of this word, I have not been able to ascertain." Its classical signification was that of a deity or superior intelligence. Its most common acceptation among the later Greeks was that of an evil spirit. Grote the historian says: "They were most frequently noticed as the causes of evil, and thus the name *demon* come to convey with it a bad sense. The objectionable ceremonies of the pagan world were defended upon the ground that in no other way could the exigencies of such mali[illegible]t beings be appeased. . . . Christian writers could easily show that not only in Homer, but in the general language of early pagans, all the gods were spoken of as demons."*

We learn from the New Testament the real character of all demons. The words *daimōn* and *daimōniōn* are there used in their variations 78 times. They are never employed to represent a holy angel, nor a departed saint, nor to signify any other than an *evil* spirit. So universal was this acceptation among Jews and Christians, that demon was one of the most reproachful epithets in vogue. Says James,

* Hist. of Greece, v. 1. c. 2.

"This wisdom descendeth not from above, but is earthly, sensual, *daimoniōdēs*," like that of demons.*

They are represented as engaged in deceiving and arraying the world against Christ. "Giving heed to doctrines of demons" involves a departure from the Christian faith. Those who were deified by the pagans and produced the highest and most deceptive order of manifestations, such as speaking in oracles and inspiring soothsayers, were no exceptions to the general character of the race. Paul doubtless refers to these when he classes evil spirits with the chief antagonists to Christianity.

"We wrestle not against flesh and blood, but against principalities against powers, against the rulers of the darkness of this world, against *ta pneumatika tēs ponērias en tois epouraniois*, wicked spirits in high or h[illegible]ly places."†

The spirit by which the damsel of Philippi was inspired, was wicked, and engaged in a forbidden work no less than those who possessed the raving demoniacs.

Demons are represented as being a source of affliction to the human family—as causing dumness, deafness, madness, palsy, and epilepsy—as trembling in view of their doom, and pleading that they might not be tormented before the time. None are excepted by the Apostle when he says: "The demons also believe and tremble."‡ "And behold they cried out, saying, what have we to do with thee,

* James, iii: 15. † Eph. 6: 12. ‡ James 2: 19.

Jesus thou son of God? art thou come hither to torment us before the time."* The translators have not represented them all as "devils," in our version of the scriptures without some very good reasons.

Tertullian, Lactantius, and Cyprian, show in what estimation they were held by the early Christians. Says Tertullian: "Hitherto, we have used words; we will now come to a demonstration of the very thing, that your Gentile gods are no one of them greater than another. For a decision of the point, let any one that is judged to be possessed by a devil be brought into open court before your tribunals; when that spirit shall be commanded by Christians to speak, he shall as truly confess himself a devil there, as elsewhere he falsely claims to be a god. Or let one equally be produced who is among you, Gentiles, *judged to be inspired by God,* who waits at your altars, and is esteemed a sacred person by you; nay, though he be actuated by one of your most venerated deities, be it Diana, the heavenly virgin, or Esculapius, who prescribes your medicines, and who pretends to relieve the dying, yet these, or any others, when they are summoned, if they dare to lie to the Christian summoning, *and if they do not confess themselves openly to be devils, then let that reproachful Christian's blood be spilt upon the spot.*"

Says Lactantius: "Nor is it a slight cause that

* Mat. 8: 29.

of the multitudes whom the *impious spirits of demons* enter, all who are healed by their expulsion adhere to the religion whose power they have experienced. These numerous causes have drawn a great multitude in a wonderful manner to God."*

REEVE, in his translation of Tertullian's Apology, quotes a remarkable note from Cyprian, pupil of the latter, and bishop of Carthage, in the third century.

CYPRIAN invited Demetrius, proconsul of Africa, to come and witness the groans and anguish of the demons who possessed human bodies, when writhing under the power with which Christians were endowed. He says: "O, if you would hear and see them when they are adjured by us, when crying out and groaning with a human voice, and feeling scourges and blows by Divine power, they *acknowledge the judgment to come*,—come and know the things which we speak are true. You will see them stand bound under our power, and you will observe them *tremble like captives!*"

Now since, as the spiritualists acknowledge, these "spirits" belong to the same family with the demons noticed in the New Testament, every argument which has been, and can be urged against the latter, is of equal force in reference to the former.

Modern usage corresponds with the New Testament signification of *demon*, and clearly indicates

* Lactantaii, Inst, lib. v. de Just., c. 22.

the vile character of the "spirits." Hence their devotees are striving to change the signification of the word.

It is to be expected that every well-informed Christian will adopt the views concerning these spirits which were sanctioned by Christ and his disciples. They will abide by the decisions of an inspired Apostle. "*I would not that ye should have fellowship with demons.* Ye *cannot* drink of the cup of the Lord, and the cup of demons: ye *cannot* be partakers of the Lord's table, and of the table of demons."*

In view of the foregoing facts, we affirm that a departed *Christian* has never manifested himself among all of these. We are fully authorized to brand as *impostor* every one of these invisible personators who have pretended to be Christ, angels and saints. We should cry *impostor* to a spirit who would represent himself as our departed father, whatever might be his proofs of identity. The idea that the abodes of bliss can be reached by the arts of necromancers and "mediums," is not to be entertained for a moment. To assert that such is the case, is virtually to contend that Satan and his agents have not only "encompassed the camp of the saints and the beloved city," but that the battle of Armageddon has been already fought, and contrary to the Apocalyptic anticipation, victory has crowned the arms of the satanic host.

1 Cor. 10: 20.

CHAPTER VII.

SPIRITUALISM IS A REVIVAL OF SORCERY.

"Neither repented they of their . . sorceries."—REV. ix: 12.

IT is so obvious and so generally believed that this intercourse is the same with the sorcery prohibited in the Bible, that no argument is necessary to prove it, in addition to what is presented in other parts of this work. We shall therefore only give a definition of terms, and the testimony of some of the most prominent spiritualists, in order to show that we do not misrepresent spiritualism.

Sorcery, magic, with craft; or divination with the assistance of evil spirits—*Webster*.

Witch, a woman who practices divination by the aid of evil spirits; one who is *possessed* with a divining spirit, or has one in her; one who exerts supernatural power by the assistance of a familiar spirit; "a medium for test personations by which the actual presence of evil spirits can be realized; a developing medium."

GOVERNOR TALMADGE says: "Now all the magic, the mysteries, the witchcraft, and necromancy of the ancient world, from the time of the Delphic Oracle, are explained by these modern investigations."—*Spiritualism, by Edmonds, vol.* 1, *p.* 422.

JUDGE EDMONDS says: "I found that both sacred and profane history was full of accounts of what we are now witnessing . . . If we may credit the traditions and private histories of the Catholic Church, it was occasionally manifest. After the Reformation, and the minds of men began to be somewhat freed from restraints which the religious domination of centuries had imposed upon them, spiritual intercourse began again to display itself. But mankind in their ignorance knew not how to deal with it. Instead of meeting the intelligence rationally, as is now done, and asking whence and why it came, it was met with prayers and fumigations, and exorcisms in a dead language; nay, with the faggot and the scaffold. About two hundred years ago, under the administration of one of the wisest of the English Judges, hundreds were tried and executed for the crime of witchcraft. The act of 1 James I, ch. xii., against witchcraft, was passed when Lord Bacon, one of the greatest minds that England has ever produced, was a member of the House of Commons, and Lord Coke, one of her most distinguished judges, was attorney general, and in the House of Lords, was referred to a committee which contained twelve bishops. And Barrington, in his observations on the statutes of 20,

Hen. VI., says that 30,000 people were burned for witchcraft within 150 years.

In our own country, too, where our sturdy ancestors planted amid savage wilds, the seeds of freedom which now so overshadows the world, it displayed itself; and *the history of Salem witchcraft is but an account of spiritual manifestations, and of man's incapacity to understand them.*"—*Spiritualism, V. I., p.* 43–44.

Allen Putnam, Unitarian clergyman and spiritualist, of Roxbury, Mass., in the *New Era* of Oct. 7th, 1854, says: "The doctrine that the oracles, soothsaying, and witchcraft of past ages, were kindred to these manifestations of our day, I for one, most fully believe."

A. J. Davis, the seer, and the *spirits* bear substantially the same testimony. He says: "I listened to Fenelon and William Ellery Channing. I was assured, also, that the time was now past when these new things would have been ignorantly termed demonism, enchantment, and witchcraft."—*Philosophy of S. Intercourse, p.* 77.

Charles Partridge, publisher of the *Spiritual Telegraph*, said to the writer—speaking of the woman of Endor—"Call her witch or what you will, *she was a medium for the spirits!*"

We asked Mr. Partridge what he deemed the strongest argument which had ever been urged against spiritualism. He replied, "Two or three texts in the Old Testament, such for instance as '*thou shalt not suffer a witch to live.*"

REV. URIAH CLARK, in the course of a lecture in Williamsburg, remarked that "Saul on one occasion became very much annoyed by the mediums, and issued a decree that they should all be put to death; but subsequently, when in trouble, he started off under cover of night, to *consult a medium!*"

It is written that "Saul had put away those that had familiar spirits, and the wizards, out of the land."

According to Mr. Clark, who is himself a medium, witches, wizards, and those who had familiar spirits, were all *mediums!*

MR. BRITTAN, Editor of the *Telegraph*, says: "If modern spiritualism is to be rejected because some of its illustrations are wanting in interest, dignity, and truth, or for the reason that they are imitated by cunning imposters, the ancient spiritualism must go with it. This is strictly legitimate, for the old Jewish phenomena were at least quite as disorderly as ours, and SIMON MAGUS *was, of all men,* PRINCE *among the workers of spiritual miracles.*"—*Review of Beecher*, p. 77.

This is sufficient to show that spiritualists deem this movement identical with sorcery. If this conclusion is correct—which we do not doubt—we should reckon as the most prominent of the ancient spiritualists,

Jannes and Jambres, Egyptian sorcerers.

Balaam, the soothsayer.

The woman of Endor.

The prophets of Baal.

The pythonic damsel of Philippi.

Elymus, the sorcerer, and

Simon Magus, the "PRINCE *among the workers of spiritual miracles.*"

The history of this noted character will serve to show with what class of persons "*Professor Brittan*" has thus instructed the public to identify himself and his spiritual fraternity.

"But there was a certain man, called Simon, which beforetime in the same city used sorcery, and bewitched the people of Samaria, giving out that himself was some great one: To whom they all gave heed, from the least to the greatest, saying, This man is the great power of God. And to him they had regard, because that of long time he had bewitched them with sorceries. But when they believed Philip preaching the things concerning the kingdom of God, and the name of Jesus Christ, they were baptized, both men and women. Then Simon himself believed also; and when he was baptized, he continued with Philip, and wondered, beholding the miracles and signs which were done. And when Simon saw that through laying on of the apostle's hands the Holy Ghost was given, he offered them money. Saying, Give me also this power, that on whomsoever I lay hands, he may receive the Holy Ghost. But Peter said unto him, Thy money perish with thee, because thou hast thought that the gift of God may be purchased with money. Thou hast neither part nor lot in this matter: for thy heart is not right in the sight of God. Repent therefore of this thy wickedness, and pray God, if perhaps the thought of thine heart may be forgiven thee. For I perceive that *thou art in the gall of bitterness, and in the bond of iniquity.*"—Acts 8: 9–23.

MOSES AND AARON BEFORE PHARAOH.

NOW AS JANNES AND JAMBRES WITHSTOOD MOSES, SO DO THESE [SPIRITUALISTS] RESIST THE TRUTH."—2 Tim. iii. 8.—*See Chapters VII and XV.*

CHAPTER VIII.

THE BOOK OF THE PROPHETS OF THE SPIRITUALISTS.

"Many false prophets are gone out into the world."—1 John iv : 1.

THE ancient false prophets were often as really inspired as the Lord's prophets, though by a widely different agency. The latter were inspired by the Divine Spirit, the former by demons.

Jehosaphat, king of Judah, joined affinity with Ahab, king of Israel. While premeditating war against Ramoth Gilead :

"Jehoshaphat said unto the king of Israel, Enquire, I pray thee, at the word of the Lord to-day. Therefore the king of Israel gathered together of prophets four hundred men, and said unto them, Shall we go to Ramoth-Gilead to battle, or shall I forbear? And they said, Go up; for God will deliver it into the king's hand. But Jehoshaphat said, *Is there* not here a prophet of the Lord besides, that we might enquire of him? And the king of Israel said unto Jehoshaphat, *There is* yet one man, by whom we may enquire of the Lord: but I hate him; for he never prophesied good unto me, but always evil: the same *is* Micaiah the son of Imla. And Jehoshaphat said, Let not the king say so. And the king of Israel called one of *his* officers, and said, Fetch quickly Micaiah the son of Imla. And the king of Israel and Jehoshaphat king of Judah sat either of them on his throne, clothed in *their* robes, and they sat in a void place at the entering in of the gate of Samaria; and all the prophets prophesied before them. And Zedekiah the son of Chenaanah had made him horns of iron, and said, Thus saith the Lord, With these thou shalt push Syria until they be consumed. And all the prophets prophesied so, saying, go up to Ramoth-gilead, and prosper: for the Lord shall deliver *it* into the hand of the king. And the messenger that went to call Micaiah spake to him, saying, Behold, the words of the prophets *declare good* to the king with one assent; let thy word therefore, I pray thee, be like one of their's, and speak thou good. And Micaiah said, *As* the Lord liveth, even what my God saith, that will I speak. And when he was come to the king, the king said unto him, Micaiah, shall we go up to Ramoth-gilead to battle, or shall I forbear? Then he said, I did see all Israel scattered upon the mountains, as sheep that have no shepherd: and the Lord said, These have no master; let them return *therefore* every man to his house in peace. And the king of Israel said to Jehoshaphat, did I not tell thee that he would not prophecy good unto me, but evil? Again he said, Therefore hear the word of the Lord; I saw the Lord sitting upon his throne, and all the host of heaven standing on his right hand and *on* his left. And the Lord said, Who shall entice Ahab king of Israel, that he may go up and fall at Ramoth-gilead? And one spake saying after this manner, and another saying after that manner. Then there came out a spirit, and stood before the Lord, and said, I will entice him. And the Lord said unto him, Wherewith? And he said, I will go out, and be a lying spirit in the mouth of all his prophets. And the *LORD* said, Thou shalt entice *him*, and thou shalt also prevail: go out, and do *even* so. Now therefore, behold, the Lord hath put a lying spirit in the mouth of these thy prophets, and the Lord hath spoken evil against thee. So the king of Israel and Jehoshaphat went up to Ramoth-gilead. And a *certain* man drew a bow at a venture, and smote the king of Israel between the joints of the harness: therefore he said to his chariot man, turn thine hand, that thou mayest carry me out of the host; for I am wounded. . . . And about the time of the sun going down he died."—2 Chron. xviii.

Here is a case of *real inspiration* of 400 prophets

by a lying spirit, by which Ahab, as a judgment for his wickedness, was deluded and fell. One prophet of God withstood them. Ahab believed the *majority*, his own flattering proteges. Jehoshaphat had no confidence in such demon-inspired prophets. Hence he inquired : "*Is there not here a prophet of the* LORD *besides, that we might inquire of him.*"

This case illustrates the principle upon which Jehovah permits men to be deceived to their ruin.

"Yea, they have chosen their own ways, and their soul delighteth in their abominations. I also will choose their delusions, and will bring their fears upon them."—Isa. lxvi: 34.

"Because they received not the love of the truth that they might be saved. And for this cause God shall send them strong delusion, that they should believe a lie: that they all might be damned who believe not the truth, but had pleasure in unrighteousness."—2 Thes. ii: 10-12.

Ahab had been a perverse man. Instead of heeding the prophets of God, he had "served Baal and worshiped him." He married Jezebel, the daughter of Ethbaal, king of the Zidonians, and reared up an altar to Baal in the house of Baal, which he had built in Samaria."* He allowed Jezebel to have Naboth murdered in order to obtain his vineyard, and committed other crimes. Therefore "The Lord said, who shall entice Ahab king of Israel, that he may go up and fall at Ramoth Gilead?" God intended he should fall, and that the false prophets whom he had patronized,

*1 Kings 16: 31-32.

should be the agents for his deception and consequent ruin.

But he was not allowed to go without a warning. A prophet of the Lord gave him all the facts in the case. Hence, when he went he went with his eyes open, and he might thank his favorite divinities and prophets for the fatal consequences of his expedition.

The damsel at Philippi, who for many days followed Paul and Silas saying, "These men are the servants of the most high God, which shew unto us the way of salvation, and who brought her masters much gain by soothsaying," was an inspired prophetess, possessed with a spirit of divination. When the spirit was cast out, her masters were angry because "the hope of their gains was gone."*

We have no reason to doubt that many persons in our times, are inspired and possessed in the same manner, and by the same class of spirits as the above-mentioned prophets and prophetesses.

Dr. DEXTER says he has "witnessed the medium so completely under the control of the spirit, that speech, motion, and even thought itself, was at the command of the spirit influencing her."†

It is well known that the seers, prophets and mediums of modern spiritualism, Messrs. Davis, Spear, Harris, Ambler, and others, profess to be inspired by finite spirits. If this be the fact—

* Acts 16: 16. † Spiritualism, p. 87.

which we have no reason to doubt—this fact identifies them as a class, with the pythonic women of Endor and Philippi, with the prophets of Baalim and Diana, and with those of heathen divinities of all ages. Their inspiration is of the same character.

There are two kinds of inspiration. One kind is effected by the Holy Spirit, the other by wicked spirits. The work of inspiration is the prerogative of God. None but the Omniscient One is competent to inspire prophets to make revelations concerning the future. The Bible does not authorize us to suppose that a righteous spirit would attempt this work. Such an one would not assume the hazardous responsibility of doing the Lord's work of inspiring a prophet on whose word was staked the weal of mortals; much less would Jehovah permit such an act by one of his children. Hence the inspiration of a prophet by a holy angel or the spirit of a saint, is a moral impossibility; and all inspiration which is not effected by the Holy Spirit, must be the work of evil spirits, and worse than useless, inasmuch as it could never be relied on, and all prophets thus inspired would be false prophets.

A better description in so few words can nowhere be found of modern inspiration and its results, according to the testimony of the spiritualists, than is given by an ancient professor of sorcery to represent the same class of phenomena in Egypt.

In the third century, Porphyry wrote an ironical letter to Anebo, an Egyptian priest, requesting information concerning divination. The letter was answered by Jamblicus, the preceptor of Anebo. In this reply occurs the following :

"Inspiration is the work neither of soul nor body, nor of their entire compound. The true cause is no other than illumination emanating from the very gods themselves, and spirits coming forth from them *and an obsession by which they hold us fully and absolutely, absorbing all our faculties even, and exterminating all human motions and operations even to consciousness itself: bringing discourses which they who utter them do not understand, but pronounce with furious lip, so that our whole being becomes secondary and subservient to the sole power of the occupying god,"*

"Some are agitated throughout the whole body, others in some of their members, others again, are entirely quiet. Sometimes there are pleasing harmonies, dances, and according-voices, and sometimes the reverse. Again, the body appears taller, or larger, or is *borne aloft through the air, or is affected by the opposite of these.*"*

"Many through divine inspiration are not burned when the fire is introduced to them, the inspiring influence preventing the fire from touching them.—Many, also, though burned, do not apprehend that

*Beecher's Essay p. 38-39—from De Myst., Sec. iii., c. 5.

they are so, because they do not then live in animal life. And some, indeed, though transfixed with spits, do not perceive it; but others that are struck on the shoulders with axes, and others that have their arms cut with knives are by no means conscious of what is done to them.

"Their energies likewise are not at all hindered. For inaccessible places become accessible to those that are divinely inspired; they are thrown into fire and over rivers, like the priest in Castabalis, without being injured; but from these things it is demonstrated that those who energize enthusiastically are *not conscious of the state they are in*, and that they neither live a human nor an animal life, according to the sense or impulse, but that they exchange this for a certain, more divine life, by which they are inspired and *perfectly possessed*."*

This description of the concomitants of ancient heathen sorcery answers so perfectly to modern spiritualism as to show that the latter is a counterpart of the former.

The spiritualists believe the same. Messrs. Edmonds, Putnam, Davis, Partridge, and Brittan testify—as we have shown in another place—that the modern phenomena are the same with the sorcery and witchcraft of former times. In doing this they have identified themselves with every class of operators in heathen sorcery. Mr. Brittan says, that *Simon Magus was a* " PRINCE " in the family.

* Taylor's Jamblicus, p. 122.

Spiritualists confess that their mediums and prophets are just as free to serve knaves and liars as any other spirits.

Rev. Allen Putnam, a spiritualist, of Roxbury, Mass., on page 57 of his recent work on the subject, speaking of the mediums and mode of communication, says, " The use of the instrument is as free to *bad* spirits as to good ones ; it has no moral nor intellectual tastes or preferences. Our wires will as readily transfer a message from one villain to his companion in villany as they will carry the most affectionate sentiment from one devout man to another. So will the aromal electricity which the spirits have learned to curb and guide, be the servant of *any spirit whatsoever.*"

Mr. Fishbough acknowledged to the writer, that the false prophets foretold by the Saviour were now in the ranks of the spiritualists. " There shall arise false Christs and false prophets, and shall show great signs and wonders, insomuch that if it were possible, they shall deceive the very elect."—Math. xxiv : 24.

It is a mistake to suppose that a man cannot be justly styled a false prophet who does not always deal in falsehoods. The man who would tell nothing but lies, would manifest as much stupidity as knavery, and have very little influence.

It is unreasonable to suppose that the 850 false prophets, who demonstrated the impotence of Baal before all Israel on mount Carmel, told nothing but lies. Their position and influence was too prominent to justify such a conclusion. For years they monopolized alike the royal patronage and the public favor. The millions of Israel heeded their counsels, adopted their system of morals and religion, and were delighted with what they deemed the inspired eloquence which flowed from their lips when moved by the patron "gods" of Israel's surrounding foes.

But what important revelation was ever made by this class of prophets? Where is it to be found? Echo answers, where? Jehovah has not deemed it proper to commemorate the sophistry of the ancient members of this family for the diversion and ruin of succeeding generations.

As might be expected, the most important of all their discoveries in this "progressive age," has been made by A. J. Davis, the "seer." It was made when attempting to vindicate his developing theory, by which he teaches that man was originally an *oyster* or a *clam* ! from which he has progressed to his present condition.

Here it is. "Flour damped with a little water, will, in a few days, or even hours, be transformed into *moving, living, feeling organism.* Any man can develope oats from rye, or *oak trees* from a combination of chesnut, pine and walnut. If oats are cast into the ground at the proper season, and kept mowed down during the summer and autumnal months, and allowed to remain undisturbed till the succeeding spring, the oats will completely disappear, and a moderate growth of rye will appear at the close of the following summer.*

If any person wishes to test the character of Mr. Davis' inspiration, it can be easily done.

Says professor Mattison, " Henceforth let no good housewife be alarmed, if, after she has prepared the flour for the oven, the loaves should suddenly turn into mud turtles, and the pies into sunfish, and move off in their respective elements. And if any of our growers of ornamental trees wish to produce the oak, and cannot well get the acorn to plant, let them take a quantity of chesnut, pine, and walnut chips, get them ground, make the meal up into little balls, and plant *them* ; and we have Mr. Davis' word for it, that from the balls will grow up *oak trees!* The farmer, also, who wants a crop of winter rye, and has not the seed, but has plenty of *oats*, has only to sow the oats in the spring, instead of rye in the fall, and the next season the moderate growth of rye will be produced ! Verily, this is not only a '*new*,' but a very *accommodating* philosophy.†

Says Rev. J. N. Murdock, Editor of the *Christian Review* : " there is only one little drawback in all this. We are impressed distinctly to say, that this whole theory, of which Mr. Davis has given us such a prelude in the above paragraph, is a fabrication. There is not a word of truth in it. The

* Approaching Crisis, p. 51. † Spirit Rapping Unveiled, p. 124.

flour is not changed to insects, the chesnut, the pine, and the walnut, do not produce the oak, and the oats are not changed to rye. If we had a boy ten years of age who could not account for the phenomena to which Mr. Davis refers, without resorting to such a theory, we should be strongly disposed to flog him for his stupidity.

"We humbly submit that a man who can conceive and deliberately print such absurdities as the above paragraph, is entitled to no confidence whatever. Yet this is the teacher on whose authority many of our citizens have surrendered their faith in the Bible; for whose crudities they have abandoned historical Christianity! In the sacred name of reason, what have they gained by the exchange? What! May God pity them and their deluded leader."

The *Mountain Cove Journal* says: "In the beginning of the orb-formation preparatory for man-formations; vehicles of the Quickening Spirit into intellectual formation, the universal concavity, and the universal convexity, were co-enfolded and encompassed in the universal zodiac, and within the concavity was the visible disclosure into the germ of the terrestrial."

The *Spiritual Harbinger* has the following:—
"In the twelfth hour, the glory of God, the life of God, the Lord of God, the Holy Proceedure, shall crown the Triune Creator with the perfect disclosive illumination. Then shall the Creator, in effulgence above the divine seraphimal, arise into the

dome of the disclosure in one comprehensive revolving galaxy of supreme Beatitudes ! !"

What superlative nonsense ! ! ! Who will say, in the face of such language, that they do not speak in a tongue, unknown to themselves and everybody else ! And these are fair specimens of hundreds of their inspired productions. The "*Spiritual Telegraph*," No. 182, says : "Ream after ream of paper has been covered with curious hieroglyphics that are perfectly useless to either the medium or circle—or, in fact, any one else—for the excellent reason that we have not thus far any CHAMPOLLION and LAYARD to interpret for us."

Says a writer :

"It would be well, perhaps, to consider the difference between Divine communications, and the supposed communication of the present time.

"Divine communications were made through 'holy men of old, who spake as they were moved by the Holy Spirit ;' these are made through infidels and sometimes knaves. The witch of Endor was certainly no match for some of those engaged in this holy (!) business.

"Divine communications were made about matters of importance, these about matters the most insignificant and trifling.

"Divine communications were made always consistent ; these are contradictory.

"Divine communications were always true ; these are generally false.

"Divine communications were not made at the option of men in general; these are made at the option of men without respect of character.

"The whole affair, beginniug, middle, and ending, is unlike anything God ever did. The removing of tables and chairs, and the 'raps,' rather indicate 'the spirits of devils working miracles,' than the work of the 'finger of God' in raising the dead, healing the sick, and doing good to fallen humanity. The work of God is like himself; the work of the devil is like himself. By their works we know them."

This class of prophets was anciently found pandering to the prejudices and desires of sinful men—detailing the minutia in the fortunes of a dupe—prophesying "smooth things," and crying peace! peace! to those whose hands were reeking with crimes of the deepest dye, and committing the greatest wrongs for the sake of gain.

Did they, by their enchantments and deceptions, gain the royal patronage, and constrain the deluded throng to replenish their coffers and laud their names? Their successors are not behind the very chiefest of them all in their zeal, absurd pretences, and delusive wiles.

Were they pronounced "false prophets?" No reliance can be placed in these! Did the Saviour declare that false prophets should show great signs and wonders, insomuch that if it were possible, they should deceive the very elect? Hundreds of our age will no doubt realize, in despair, that his words are true.

The faithful man of God who possesses the Scriptures is "*thoroughly furnished unto all good works.*"* "The word of His grace," says Paul, "is able to build you up, and give you an inheritance among them which are sanctified."† Hence we are not authorized to expect any Divinely inspired revelation in addition to the Bible.

On the other hand, the Old Testament cautions us against necromancers, and false prophets, and "adding unto his words;" and the New Testament warns us against the insidious wiles of "deceivers," "false Christs," "false prophets," "seducing spirits," "doctrines of devils," and "lying wonders." Hence we infer that the great danger lies not in any liability to reject any recent Divine revelation, but in a liability to receive spurious communications on the authority of "lying wonders."

We are thankful for the Holy Bible as a standard of appeal. While others may choose the revelations of heathen divinities, and departed spirits, let *us* have the "*living oracles.*" Theirs of the past are revelations lost and forgotten: ours are those which have survived the conflicts and revolutions of ages. Theirs of the present are such as must perish with their dupes and the enemies of Jehovah. But ours must endure when the heavens and earth shall pass away.

* 2 Tim. iii:16, 17. † Acts xx: 32.

CHAPTER IX.

ANCIENT ORACLES OF THE SPIRITUALISTS

"Shew the things that are to come hereafter, that we may know that ye are gods."—ISA. xli: 23.

"THERE were many places in Greece where oracles were delivered. The most ancient and most celebrated of these were attached to the sanctuaries of Zeus and Apollo, at Dodona and Delphi.

Herodotus says, that Dodona was by far the most ancient of the Grecian oracles; and tells us on the authority of Egyptian priests, that it was founded by a priestess, whom the Phœnicians had carried away from Thebes in Egypt, giving also another version of the story related to him by the priestesses of Dodona—but indeed of the same import. In confirmation of this narrative, he tells us that the two oracles of Egyptian Thebes and Dodona resembled each other entirely, and hence draws the conclusion that the art of divination as practised in his time in Greece, was derived from Egypt.*

* Lib. ii., c. 58.

The oracle of Delphi vied with that of Dodona in the truth and perspicuity of its answers, but surpassed the latter by far, in magnificence and wealth. The place in which the oracles were delivered was called Pythium, and the priestess who consulted the god, was named Pythia.*

Diodorus relates that there was a cave on Parnassus, whence rose an exhalation that caused the goats to leap and skip about, and which intoxicated the brain.† A shepherd having approached it, to learn the cause of so extraordinary an effect, was immediately seized with a violent agitation of his frame, and pronounced words which, though unintelligible to himself, revealed future events. Others having experienced the same effects, rumors of it were soon spread throughout the neighborhood. The cave was no more approached without great awe. The exhalation was deemed to have something supernatural in it. A priestess was appointed for the reception of its wonderful effects, and a tripod placed over the vent.‡ The priestess was seated on the tripod, when she pronounced the

* From *Pytho*, a serpent—as Apollo was said to have killed a very large one at the mouth of the cave. † Diod. Dic., Lib. xvi.

‡ What kind of a machine this celebrated tripod was, has caused much inquiry by the ancient antiquarians—but without leading to any certain result. Some consider it to have been a brass vessel through which a miraculous vapor was conveyed into the belly of the priestess, and then came out of her mouth; others say that it was large enough to plunge herself into it. But these are all mere conjectures. It was called tripod because it had three feet.

answers of the god. A temple to Apollo was erected near the cave, and the city of Delphi rose by degrees in its vicinity.

At first a single priestess or Pythia, was sufficient to answer those who came to consult the oracle, as they were then few in number; but in the course of time its reputation rose, and the applications for advice became more frequent. Two Pythias were then appointed to mount the tripod alternately with each other, and still a third was chosen as a substitute in case of death.

When Pythia had to consult the god, which at first could only take place at a certain period in each year, but afterwards every month, she had to prepare herself for that purpose by sacrifices, purification, and a three days' fast. Then, having washed herself in the fountian of Castalia, at the foot of Parnassus, and shaken the laurel tree that grew by it, she crowned herself with a garland of those leaves, and sometimes even swallowed a portion of them. Then she seated herself on the tripod, and waited for the impulse of the god as it was called. As soon as she had received the divine afflatus she began to swell, her hair rose, her looks grew wild, her mouth foamed, a sudden and violent trembling seized her whole body with all the symptoms of distraction and frenzy. Sometimes the paroxysm was so terrible, that the priests as well as the consulters, withdrew from fear; and once it caused the death of Pythia, as we are told by Plutarch. The report even spread abroad that a dragon or serpent had been seen to return the answer from under the tripod, and that one priestess was killed by the monster. Sometimes, however, the mind of the Pythia was but gently moved. She uttered at intervals some words almost inarticulate, which the priests or prophets carefully collected and arranged with some degree of order and connection. At last she was conducted to her private apartment, where she generally remained in quietude for several days, ere she could after this violent excitement and fatigue, recover her usual strength. But Lucan says that sudden death was frequently either a reward or punishment from the god, whose inspiration she had received.

Though the prophets were assisted by poets to reduce the answer to verses, the composition was, however, commonly so rude, that it gave occasion for scoffers to remark, how very surprising it was that Apollo, who presided over the choir of the muses, should deliver his answers to Pythia in such miserable verse. The oracles were also often given in prose.

The oracular answers were generally embodied in ambiguous language, admitting of opposite meanings. It is, however, conceded that they were sometimes perspicuous, and not to be misunderstood; and that they nevertheless appear to have predicted what afterwards actually took place." —*Hebbe's Hist., vol.* 3, *p.* 38–43.

CICERO says:

"I now come to you, Apollo,
Monarch of the sacred centre of the
Great world, full of thy inspiration;
The Pythian priestesses proclaim
Thy prophecies.

For Chryspus has filled an entire volume with your oracles, many of which, as I said before, I consider utterly false, and many others only true by accident, as often happens in any common conversation. Others, again, are so obscure and involved, that their very interpreters have need of other interpreters; and the decisions of one lot have to be referred to other lots. Another portion of them are so ambiguous that they require to be analyzed by the logic of dilectitions.

"Thus when Fortune uttered the following oracle respecting Crœsus, the richest king of Asia,

'When Crœsus has the Halys cross'd,
A mighty kingdom will be lost,'

that monarch expected he should ruin the power of his enemies; but the empire that he ruined was his own. And which ever result had ensued, the oracle would have been true!" [Cicero on Divination, sec. 56.]

"The same ambiguity attends the famous reply of the same oracle to Pyrrhus:

'I do pronounce that Rome
Pyrrhus shall overcome;'

which may be interpreted to mean, either that Rome

should overcome Pyrrhus, or that Pyrrhus should overcome Rome. Whoever reads Herodotus and Pausanias carefully, will find most of their oracles—and they record a great many—either so dark as to be unintelligible, or so equivocal as to bear whatever interpretation policy might be pleased to impose upon them." [Calmet's Dic.]

Herodotus informs us that "Crœsus, King of Lydia, alarmed at the growing power of Cyrus, King of Persia, and meditating an attack on his dominions, was anxious first to consult the most celebrated oracles as to the issue of such an important enterprise, before he committed himself to it. Prior, however, to his submitting to the oracle the important question upon which his fate depended, he determined to propound one which should enable him, as he thought, to test the prescience of the oracle. He accordingly sent messengers to Delphi, and, having carefully considered the period required for the journey, and allowed them ample time, he commanded them at the appointed hour to present themselves before the Pythoness, and propose this question: 'What is Crœsus, son of Alyattes, now doing?' They were to write the answer carefully down, and send it to him. The answer was to this effect:

'I count the sand, I measure out the sea;
The silent and the dumb are heard by me.
E'en now the odors to my sense that rise,
A tortoise boiling with a lamb supplies,
Where brass below and brass above it lies.'

The fact was that Crœsus, determined to be occupied in the most unlikely and unkingly manner, was engaged at that time in boiling the flesh of a tortoise and a lamb together in a covered vessel of brass.

Crœsus was so impressed with the exactness of this response, that he determined to do all in his power to propitiate this oracle, and to trust himself to its direction. He accordingly sent to Delphi the most costly presents in gold and silver—amounting altogether, according to the computation of the Abbe Barthelemy, to £879,547—with orders to make the following inquiry: "Crœsus, sovereign of Lydia and of various nations, esteems these the only genuine oracles. In return for the sagacity which has marked your declarations, he sends these proofs of his liberality. He finally desires to know whether he may proceed against the Persians, and whether he shall require the assistance of any allies." The answer was, that if Crœsus carried his arms against the Persians, he would overthrow a great empire; and that he would do well to make alliances with the most powerful states of Greece. Interpreting this reply to his own advantage, but anxious to put the case in another aspect before the oracle, he sent a third time, to inquire as to the duration of his empire. The answer on that occasion was:

"When o'er the Medes a mule shall sit on high,
O'er pebbly Hermus then, soft Lydian, fly—

Fly with all haste, for safety scorn thy fame;
Nor scruple to deserve a coward's name."

Still giving to the answers of the oracle the interpretation most favorable to himself, Crœsus regarded the reign of a mule over Media as an impossibility, and thence inferred the stability of his own power. Under this impression he made war on Persia, and, as is well known, was soon vanquished, stripped of his dominions, condemned to death, but ultimately preserved and supported as a captive by Cyrus."—*Gentile Nations.*

This revelation to Crœsus stands at the head of all responses from any heathen oracles. This, and that of Ahab's four hundred prophets, are the best feats ever performed by sorcerers. Both are fine illustrations of this sort of divination and its consequences. They are far superior to any revelation of modern spiritualism; though doubtless effected by the same class of agencies.

Now what is ever gained by consulting familiar spirits? Neither Ahab nor Crœsus could obtain any but deceptive information concerning the future. The former lost his life. The latter gave $4,397,235 to be duped—styled a mule—be stripped of his dominions, and condemned to death!

Nothing better can ever be expected from such a source. If spiritualists, by hundreds, do not realize a similar fate at the hands of the demons, it will be only because opportunities are wanting for such a result. May the Author of *the living oracles* ever preserve us all from such calamities!

CHAPTER X.

SATANIC AND DEMONIAC MIRACLES.

They "shall shew great signs and wonders; insomuch that, if it were possible, they shall deceive the very elect."—MATH. xxiv: 24

As sorcery had been for a long time discarded as a matter of mere pretence, or at most as another name for jugglery, most persons were unprepared to expect anything really wonderful from its revival. When such persons witness a spiritual sign they are inclined to impute it to "the great power of God." Hence they are the readiest dupes of the spirits and their mediums, and the greatest number of proselytes to modern sorcery have been from this class. It seems necessary, therefore, in order to be properly on our guard, to understand what signs may be expected from this source.

I shall be met at the outset with the oft-repeated assertion that "spiritualists pretend to work miracles which they never perform." This is undoubtedly true of sorcerers in every age. Thus we find in Taylor's Jamblichus, page 220, the following curious note "from a rare Greek manuscript of Psellus on *demons*, according to the dogmas of the Greeks," written in the tenth century.

"GOETIA, or *witchcraft*, is a certain art respecting material and *terrestrial demons*, whose images it causes to become visible to the spectators of this art. And some of these demons it leads up, as it were, from Hades, but others it draws down from on high: and these, too, such as are of an *evil species*. This art, therefore, causes certain phantastic images to appear before the spectators. And before the eyes of some, indeed, it pours exuberant streams; but to others it promises freedom from bonds, delicacies and favors. They draw down, too, powers of this kind by songs and incantations.

But MAGIC, according to the Greeks, is a thing of a very powerful nature. For they say that this forms the *last* part of the sacerdotal science. MAGIC, indeed, investigates the nature, power and quality of everything sublunary; viz: of the elements and their parts, of animals, all various plants and their fruits, of stones and herbs; and in short, it explores the essence and power of everything. From hence, therefore, it produces its effects. And it forms *statues* which procure health, make all various figures and things, which become the instruments of disease. . . Often, too, *celestial fire* is made to appear through magic, and then statues laugh and lamps are spontaneously enkindled."

A more remarkable passage occurs in the First

Book of the Metamorphosis of Apuleius, written in the second century:

"By magical incantations rapid rivers may be made to run back to their fountains, the sea be congealed, winds become destitute of spirit, the sun be held back in its course, the moon be forced to scatter her foam, the stars be torn from their orbits, the day be taken away, and the night be detained."*

From the foregoing is it not obvious that the sorcerers on behalf of whom Psellus and Apuleius wrote, were guilty of a religious theft, in ascribing the most remarkable miracles of the Mosaic dispensation to "evil" spirits and their own sinful arts?

It is clear that reference is here made to the miraculous darkness in Egypt, the dividing and "congealing"† of the Red Sea, the flowing back of Jordan, the lengthening of the day in the time of Joshua, the descent of fire on Sinai and Carmel, the impotence of the Chaldean furnace, and the stilling of the tempest by the Redeemer. All of these with some others are imputed to magic!

It appears that the French infidels were not the first nor the last to teach that Moses and the Messiah were magicians! A perverseness of this character can be traced throughout the entire history of sorcery, from its climax in Egypt, to the most puerile manifestations of modern spiritualism. It seems to have been natural for the entire family

* Taylor's Jamblichus, p. 222. † Exodus xv: 8.

of every age, either to ascribe the greatest of God's miracles to their "*demons of an evil species*" or to deny them altogether. Perhaps we have no reason to expect anything better as the natural consequence of the occupation of these pretenders to Divine power.

The magicians of Egypt ascribed the signs which were wrought by Jehovah to the same agencies as their own, till, as the result of a miracle which they were unable to counterfeit, they were constrained to confess their perverseness, exclaiming, "*This is the finger of God!*"

Simon Magus, the noted sorcerer of Samaria, taught the people that his wonders were effected by Divine power. Hence, "They all gave heed from the least to the greatest, saying this man is the great power of God."

The confessed successors of these ancient masters are emulating their example. They contend that their miracles and inspiration are the same in character, and effected by the same class of agencies as those of Christ, the Apostles and prophets, all must redound to the honor of departed spirits!

The spiritualists will do well to bear in mind what is observable in our first quotation—that the wonders of sorcery and magic according to the dogmas of the Greeks, are all to be imputed to "evil demons." They very well understood that sorcerers could obtain assistance from no other spirits than those of an "*evil species.*"

But notwithstanding all the religious thefts, the false assumptions and extravagant pretences of sorcerers, they have really performed signs, though of a low order; and we are authorized by the Bible to expect this from their successors of our own times.

"And Moses and Aaron went in unto Pharaoh, and they did so as the Lord had commanded: and Aaron cast down his rod before Pharaoh, and before his servants, and it became a serpent. Then Pharaoh also called the wise men and the sorcerers: now the magicians of Egypt, *they also did in like manner with their enchantments. For they cast down every man his rod, and they became serpents: but Aaron's rod swallowed up their rods.* * * And Moses and Aaron did so, as the Lord commanded; and he lifted up the rod, and smote the waters that *were* in the river, in the sight of Pharaoh, and in the sight of his servants; and all the waters that *were* in the river were turned to blood. *And the magicians of Egypt did so with their enchantments:* * * And Aaron stretched out his hand over the waters of Egypt; and the frogs came up, and covered the land of Egypt. *And the magicians did so with their enchantments, and brought up frogs upon the land of Egypt.* * * Aaron stretched out his hand with his rod, and smote the dust of the earth, and it became lice in man, and in beast; all the dust of the land became lice throughout all the land of Egypt. And the magicians did so with their enchantments to bring forth lice, but they could not: so there were lice upon man, and upon beast. Then the magicians said unto Pharaoh, *This is the finger of God.*" —Ex. vii: viii.

Says Dr. Cumming, of London: "Whatever God does in the world, satan always gets up something very like it, because his hope of progress is by deception. We may quote the miracles of the magicians of Egypt: satan got up his miracles too, perhaps real, at least supernatural ones. When there were true prophets, Satan had his company of prophets, too. When God was manifest in the flesh, which was one thousand eight hundred and fifty-one years ago, satan was manifest in the flesh too : he got up a mimicry—demoniacal possessions. We find the same fact now-a-days ; for as God manifest in the flesh was the truth that seems to have struck satan down, so the preaching of this truth strikes down satan still. Rhennius had the idea that among many of the Indians there is something approaching to demoniac possessions. And missionaries declare that they sometimes find manifested among the heathen, the unconverted savages of the desert, a power that is all but superhuman ; so that whenever the gospel is preached in heathen lands, there is always a desperate effort to crush and extinguish it. My opinion of the church of Rome is, that it is one colossal demoniac possession. I know that certain men look on it merely as a corrupt church, a church a little astray. I am not denying that there are good men in that church in spite of it ; but this I do say, and persist in, that the system seems to me one huge demoniacal possession, where satan has his license and his miracles. I believe that many of the miracles wrought by priests in the middle ages were supernatural, or infranatural rather. Whenever I hear a priest say, 'We have wrought miracles,' I admit it. I say certainly you have. I do not doubt it. If you had not done them, you would have lost one of the brands by which your church is distinguished.' I believe that that system of apostacy is just the counterpart to the true church ; and no man can fail to notice, 'throughout the book of Revelation,' how the two great opposing bodies are, the Lamb and the wife of the Lamb, and they that are his, and the 'beast' of the apostacy, and they that belong to him and are his."*

"And he doeth *great wonders*, so that he maketh fire come down from heaven on the earth in the sight of men, and deceiveth them that dwell on the earth by *the means of those miracles* which he had power to do in the sight of the beast."†

"And the devil, taking him up into an high mountain, shewed unto him all the kingdoms of the world in a moment of time . . . And he brought him to Jerusalem and set him on a pinnacle of the temple, and said unto him, If thou be the son of God, cast thyself down from hence."‡

It is written that "False Christs and false prophets shall shew *great signs and wonders*, insomuch that, if it were possible, they shall deceive the very elect."§

"That man of sin, the son of perdition," was to be revealed "after the working of satan with *all power and signs and lying wonders*, and with all the dceivableness of unrighteousness in them that perish.||"

* Cumming on Miracles, pp. 243–244. † Rev. 13; 13.
‡ Luke 4: 5, 9. § Mat. 24: 24. || 2 Thes. 2: 1, 10.

And finally, manifestations are to be expected from "the spirits of devils, [*demons*] *working miracles* which go forth unto the kings of the earth and of the whole world, to gather them to the battle of that great day of God Almighty."*

"'Twas by an order from the Lord
The ancient prophets spoke his word;
His Spirit did their tongues inspire,
And warm their hearts with heavenly fire.

Great God! mine eyes with pleasure look
On the dear volume of thy book:
There my Redeemer's face I see,
And read his name who died for me.

Let the false raptures of the mind
Be lost and vanish in the wind;
Here I can fix my hope secure;
This is thy word—and must endure."

*Rev. 16: 14.

CHAPTER XI.

SPIRITUALISM IS REVIVING POLYTHEISM.

"And it shall be, if thou do at all forget the Lord thy God, and walk after other gods, and serve them, and worship them; I testify against you this day, that ye shall surely perish."—DEUT. viii: 19.

THE gods of the Pagans were the spirits of the dead. As evidence of this, the most of their images were made to resemble the human form in some respects; and many of them were the very likeness of human beings.

They were represented as possessing the qualities, appetites, desires, and dispositions of men.

> "Gods partial, changeful, passionate, unjust,
> Whose attributes were rage, revenge and lust."

"This was the natural consequence of their origin. Having once animated human bodies, and being supposed still to retain human passions and appetites, they were believed, in their state of deification, to feel the same sensual desires which they had felt on earth ; and to pursue the same means for their gratification."*

Mr. Farmer, in his elaborate work on the worship of human spirits, finds that worship first in Egypt, where it became deeply rooted ; and from thence spread among all the nations of the earth. He says the twelve great gods of Egypt, as well as the CARBIRI of Phœnecia, were dead men deified. He believes these were the *immediate objects of worship* by both of those nations. In his various and extensive researches, he traces the worship of departed spirits from these nations to the Assyrians, Syrians, Chaldeans, Babylonians, Arabians, Greeks and Romans. He says, "That the gods of Greece and Rome were derived from Egypt and Phœnecia, is so universally known, that it is needless to multiply quotations in order to prove that Polytheism, among the Greeks and Romans, was the same with that which we have traced in more ancient nations." "The deification of departed heroes and of statesmen was that which in all probability introduced the universal belief of material and tutelar gods, as well as the practice of worshiping those gods through the medium of a statue cut in a human figure." He has adduced a great number of testimonies and facts to show that the worship of human spirits prevailed among the Scythians, Massagetes, Getes, the Goths, Germans, Persians, Arabians and

* Ency. Brit., Art. Polytheism.

the inhabitants of Meroe. He says, "You may find everywhere throughout the whole world one uniform law and opinion, that there is one GOD, the King and Father of all; and many gods, the sons of God, who reign on earth."

Nothing appears more certain than that the gods of the Greeks, usually styled demons, were the spirits of the dead. Says GROTE, "The demons first introduced into the religious atmosphere of the Grecian world by the author of weeks and days [Hesiod] are always deserving of attention as the seed of a doctrine which afterwards underwent many changes and became of great importance; first as the constituent element of the Pagan faith, then as one of the helps of its subversion. . . The objectionable ceremonies of the Pagan world were defended upon the ground that in no other way could the exigencies of such malignant beings be appeased. They were most frequently noticed as causes of evil, and thus the name [dæmon) came insensibly to convey with it a bad sense; the idea of an evil being as contrasted with the goodness of a god. So it was found by Christian writers when they commenced their controversy with Paganism; one branch of their argument led them to identify the Pagan gods with demons in the evil sense, and the insensible change in the received meaning of the word lent them assistance. *For they could easily show that not only in Homer, but in the gene-*

ral language of early Pagans, all the gods were spoken of as demons."*

Says Dr. Hebbe: "Eternal existence was not a quality admitted to belong to the gods of Greece; nor were they represented as the first and original gods. According to the earliest views of the Greeks, the gods often wandered among them, shared in their business, requited them with good or ill, in conformity to their reception."

"Noah was the original Zeus and Dios of the Greeks. He was a planter of the vine, and inventor of fermented liquors—hence *Zeuth* ferment—rendered Zeus by the Greeks. Bacchus was Chus, the grandson of Noah. Ammon was Ham."†

"Hesiod taught that 'The spirits of departed mortals become *demons* when separated from their earthly bodies;' and PLUTARCH, that 'The dėmons of the Greeks were the *ghosts* and *genii* of departed men.' 'All Pagan antiquity affirms,' says Dr. CAMPBELL, 'that from Titan and Saturn, the poetic progeny of Cœlus and Terra, down to Æsculapius, Proteus, and Minos, all their *divinities* were the *ghosts* of dead men; and were so regarded by the most erudite of the Pagans themselves."

HESIOD thus beautifully expresses their views:

"The gods who dwell on high Olympus' hill,
First framed a golden race of men, who lived
Under old Saturn's calm, auspicious sway;

* Grote's Hist. of Greece, vol. 1, c. 2.

† See Ency. Brit., Art. Polytheism; also Cyclo. Philadelphia ed., Art. Demon.

> Like gods they lived, their hearts devoid of care,
> Beyond the reach of pain and piercing woes,
> The infirmities of age, nor felt nor feared,
> Their nerves with youthful vigor strong, their days
> In jocund mirth they past remote from ills.
> Now when this godlike race were lodg'd on earth,
> By Jove's high will to demigods they rose,
> And airy demons who benign on earth
> Converse, the guides and guardians of mankind.
> In darkness veiled they range earth's utmost bound.
> This reward from beauteous Jove awaits illustrious deeds."

VIRGIL represents Magnus Apollo as bending from the sky to address the youth Julius: "Go on, spotless boy, in the paths of virtue, it is the way to the stars; offspring of the gods thyself, so shalt thou become the father of gods."

When Paul preached Jesus and the Resurrection, at Athens, he was accused of setting forth strange *daimonia*, demons. To this he replied: "Athenians! I perceive that you are—*deisidaimonesterous*—exceedingly devoted to the worship of demons. For as I passed by and beheld your devotions, I found an altar with this inscription: TO AN UNKNOWN GOD." But how did this prove them exceedingly devoted to the worship of demons? Plainly, *all* their gods were *demons*, and they worshiped not only all they knew, but one whom they knew not.* Says Paul, "the things which the Gentiles sacrifice, they sacrifice to *demons*, not to God.†

* Acts 17: 18. † 1 Cor. 10: 20.

JOSEPHUS represents the daughters of the Midianites, when in obedience to the advice and direction of Balaam, they were endeavoring to seduce the Israelites to the worship of their gods, as using the following language: "*You should worship the proper gods of the country, especially while our gods are common to all men*, and yours such as belong to nobody else but yourselves."* What those proper gods of the country were who were "*common to all men*," may be learned from the Bible. The Israelites were seduced by the wiles of the Midianites to the worship of their divinities, in consequence of which twenty-four thousand of the Israelites died of the plague. It is said of the daughters of Moab—

"They called the people unto the sacrifices of their gods: and the people did eat, and bowed down to their gods. And Israel joined himself unto Baal-peor: and the anger of the Lord was kindled against Israel. And those that died in the plague were twenty and four thousand."—Num. xxv: 2, 9.

The psalmist says, "they joined themselves unto Baal-peor, and *ate the sacrifices of the dead*."†

The foregoing is sufficient to establish the fact that the gods of the heathen nations, which the Midianites declared were "*common to all men*," were no others than *dead men deified*.

It is a mistake to suppose that the heathen worshiped wood and stone *solely* in their images. The

* Josephus b. iv, c. vi.

† Ps. 106: 28.

images were considered only as representatives of their deities, which were supposed to dwell in or about them.

Says Dr. Hebbe: "The form given to the deities of the East was only considered as a means to represent them to the senses. 'It was,' says Mr. Heeren, 'never any more, and this is the reason why no hesitation was made among the Eastern nations to depart from the human form, and to disfigure it wherever it seemed possible to give, by that means, a greater degree of distinctness to the symbolic representation, or if any other object, could thus be successfully accomplished."—*Ancient Greece, p.* 55.

Says Mr. Beecher: "The Jews before Christ, and the Fathers after, believed that evil departed spirits lurked in images, spoke in oracles, controlled omens, and in various ways encouraged men to worship them.*

Taylor in his translation of Jamblichus, p. 39, when speaking of the sacred animals of the Egyptians, inserts the following note from Plutarch's treatise of Isis and Osiris:

"Hence the divinity is not worse *represented* in these animals than in the workmanships of copper and stone, which in a similar manner suffer corruption and decay, but are naturally deprived of all sense and consciousness. This then I consider as

* Essay, p. 49.

the best defence that can be given of the adoration of animals by the Egyptians."

Paul says: "The idol," i. e. the *image*, "is nothing." The sacrifices of the Gentiles were made "to *demons*"—spirits that were believed to dwell in and about the images which represented them.

"The Sandwich Islanders, when they found that Christians supposed they worshipped the images of their gods, were much amused, and said, 'We are not such fools.' They used the idol as an aid to fix their minds on their divinity. Some of them supposed their divinity was a spirit residing in their idol."*

Spirits and their Followers Inculcate Polytheism.

Says Mr. Beecher, "Invoking the presence of many mediators, they revive the essential elements of both Pagan and Papal apostacy; denying the one Mediator Christ, by whose blood alone we live and by whom we approach unto God."†

When Mr. Spear, of Boston, was pronouncing his inspired benediction on Mrs. Mettler, of Hartford, on the 30th of January, 1853, the inspiring spirit made him say: "Deity of deities, thy wills be done on the earth as they are done in the Heaven of heavens."‡ If a plurality of gods is not taught here we do not understand language.

*Bliss on the Apocalypse, p. 260.

† Essay, p. 73.

‡ Fowler's Essay.

MR. EDWARD J. MATTHEWS says, in the *Spiritual Telegraph*, No. 178, that he wrote the following "*by inspiration*:"

"'God,' 'the Infinite!' two distinct terms, but alas! how misunderstood!—how interconfused in their signification, alike by the theologian and the philosopher!

When we look back into the history of the term 'God,' we soon discover that giving unto God the attribute of infinity in any respect whatever, is of recent origin compared to the origin of the usage of the term 'God' or 'gods.'

The idea attaching itself to the word 'God' was first of all 'guardian spirit,' and as different nations were very properly supposed to have different guardian spirits, so did the Jews speak of 'Jehovah,' their 'guardian spirit,' as being their God, and spoke of the gods of other nations as being 'strange gods.' But though acknowledging 'strange gods' (consequently a plurality of gods,) they denied the attribute of infinity to all except their own God, 'Jehovah.' That the Jews believed in a plurality of gods is evident from the fact that the Hebrew Scriptures commence with, 'In the beginning the GODS (ELOHIM) created the heavens and the earth.' And again, 'The GODS said, Let US create man,' etc.

The ancient Greeks and Romans believed in a plurality of gods, who were, in their opinion, spiritual beings who ruled over the affairs of this earth, and who were of different degrees of power and development. Some had power to produce or develop new forms of being on this earth; others could only influence or (psychologize) the minds of men; some had power over the different forces of nature, and others (genii) were merely attached to different private families.

But in all these, in my opinion, very sensible and consistent conceptions of the gods, they never attached the idea of infinity to any of them, except to one being, for whom they had no name, whom they called '*Deus summus*,' '*Deus optimus et maximus*,' etc., the ruler and controller of all things, from whom all things existed, and about whom, by virtue of his infinite nature, nothing could ever be known.

Far more sensible, it appears to me, is the above idea of the nature of 'ELOHIM, the gods,' than that of modern orthodoxy, which arrogantly asserts the absurd doctrine of *special providences* from an *infinite God.*

If special providences do occur, they come from some special guardian spirit or god, but not an infinite one; for the infinite can only act by universal laws.

If prayer is to be offered to God, it is absurd to suppose that the Infinite can be moved by our petitions; it is only a finite god or guardian spirit that can be so influenced.

The existence of all things in the universe proves the existence of an Infinite Being, and that one of infinite power and intelligence, from whom 'all things flow ;' but who must necessarily be incapable of doing finite acts. The very existence of a finite act shows that it was conceived and done by a finite being. The creation or development of man, and the different races of plants and animals, as they are on this globe, is a finite act, and therefore the work of finite gods. The progression of the different races and families of men on this earth, are doubtless influenced by different gods, and some of them of very different dispositions from each other, but all of them under the control of still higher gods, such, for example, as the great Spirit or guardian God of this earth, or rather, perhaps, a circle of guardian gods for this earth.

Again ; as we progress, may we not be attracting still higher gods to this earth ? and may not this present spiritual movement be caused by this higher influence pouring down upon us from still higher spheres ?

It has of late been fashionable with some, who have perceived the absurdity of praying to an infinite God, to decry the use of prayer altogether. But this is going to the opposite extreme. I believe in praying most fervently, both by action (without which prayer is a mockery) and by raising up our hearts and minds to the gods, as I believe that the gods are but finite beings and capable of being influenced by mental emotion. Pray, pray, I say, intensely to the highest *guardian spirit* or *god* that can benefit you. While working actively in all the duties of life, pray for higher spiritual wisdom, and you will have it. Are you in misfortune? The kind and loving sympathy of a guardian God is to be had for the asking.

Hoping that the above suggestion will influence some of your readers to disconnect the terms 'God' and 'the Infinite,' and thus have some realizing sense of the sources of special providences.

I remain your sincere friend for progression,

EDWARD J. MATTHEWS.

HOMER, N. Y., *Sept.* 15, 1855.

A spirit pretending to be "*God's High and Holy Spirit, formerly Jesus of Nazareth,*" through M. L. Arnold, says: "Come unto me all ye heavy laden, and I will give you rest. * * Come then and be saved by God's Infinite Mercy.

"The first thing I call on you for is your heart. Unless you give me your heart, you *cannot do me any good, nor advance your own salvation.*" Man's acts cannot be foreseen by God, as far as these acts are the acts of his will." "The seventh circle is so perfectly one with him that they know all that God knows." "The only similarity wanting to make man God is infinity." "I am a high spirit—I am the Son of God." "Advice and aid will be freely rendered to all who serve and obey God; or, *what is the same, his Holy Spirits!*"*

* Origin of All Things pp. 82, 70, 61, 19' 22, 18, 43.

The spirit of J. P. Greaves, through William North, says: "*There is no Supreme Spirit.* * * A personal God, is but one of an infinite spirit-world. *Each spirit is a God.* * * No spirit was ever created by another, or came into existence of itself. Every spirit is eternal, indestructible, and indivisible in essence, *infinite in potence.* * * *Polytheism is, on the one hand, a like impersonation of various forms of perfection in the abstract. On the other hand, the deification of heroes and sages is no delusion, but a true instinct of their innate greatness and future glory in advanced conditions of being.* * * *Man is his own maker and his own judge."—Nichols' Magazine, Jan.* 1855.

Mr. JONATHAN KOONS, of Athens Co., Ohio, writing to the *Spiritual Universe*, under date of Nov. 10, 1854, says the spirits teach in his noted spirit-room, that "*Divinity* commences with the first degree of developed *human spirits*; from which degree of *Divine* intelligence, the *Divine minds* become successively involved into higher *generated* elementary conditions, and connecting influences, which give rise to a chain of higher degrees of *Divine* intelligences, and Deifications, until all flow together into a positive *Divine* unanimity of mind; into a *joint ruling God-head.* And as many drops of water compose a lake, so, also, many personal spirit individualities compose a joint ruling principle in the highest spheres of intelligence."

The Jehovah is only a council of dead men ! !

PAINE, the noted infidel, has been honored with a seat among the highest authorities, and in some respects, bears the palm among these heathen deities. His own account of his "Pilgrimage," which he has communicated through some medium, is placed at the head of the list, and constitutes the first chapter in modern demon-biography. Messrs. PARTRIDGE and BRITTAN have honored him with a publication of his "Philosophy of Creation."

We have been informed by reliable authority, that a spirit who indulges in profane language occasionally, and who subscribes himself alternately, "Devil," and "Tom Paine," proclaims himself to be the only God in existence!

It is the avowed purpose of the spiritualists to subvert Christianity and establish their own religion on its ruins.

"THE NEW THEOLOGY.—It cannot escape the observation of any individual, who will carefully note the movements and signs of the times, that there is a new system of theological teaching arising in the world to take the place of the old and threadbare doctrines which have constituted the essence of popular religion. * * Yet, though the theology which has been long cherished and defended by the Church, is fast growing old, and is even now ready to vanish away, there exists an urgent necessity on the part of the true reformer *to make his arm strong for its final overthrow and extinction."—Ambler's Messenger, No.* 7.

Mr. Brittan says: "The age is pregnant with mighty revolutions, which are destined to shake the political and religious institutions of the world. The old theological forms and organisms have well nigh answered the end of their being. . . Their existence must soon terminate, for the mission of sectarianism is about to close. . . All existing religious formulas tend to restrict the mental freedom and spiritual development of man. They are, therefore, unsuited to the present age, and by a law which will admit of no exceptions, they must go back, and mingle with the elements of dissolved and forgotten things. . . We must have a church whose ministers shall be employed to illustrate the philosophy of the material and spiritual universes, and to instruct the people in the true science of life. . . The members must be drawn together by the principle of spiritual attraction. The union, if real and permanent, will result from the *natural affinities*."*

If we understand this language, it teaches that the present religious denominations are to be speedily supplanted by this spiritualistic sect. They are generally deficient in those elements of character which constitute devout Christians, and are destitute of that charity which tempers Christian associations, furnishes their chief bond of union, and is possessed by those only who have been converted to Christ. Without *this* all pretensions to religion

* Review of Butler, pp. 61, 62.

are no better than "a sounding brass and a tinkling cymbal."

Hence their aversion to the Christian religion, and their anxiety for a church with such a "union" as "will result from *natural affinities*;" not from conversion to Christ.

Mr. Fishbough stated in a public meeting that he "regretted the too general absence of the religious element among the spiritualists, in consequence of which their fraternity is but a 'ball of sand.'"

Spiritualists worship the creature more than the Creator.

Do they deny this? Has not intercourse with the dead had this result in all ages? Is it not its natural fruit? Do they not devote their time, talents, means, and influence to the service of the spirits? Do not the spirits claim the *wills* of their votaries, and do not all of the mediums submit theirs before they can be "developed?" Do they not *believe* the spirits, even when they contradict the Bible? Do they not observe their instructions as their rule of faith and practice? Do they not render to them such devotion and service as the spirits demand? Do they not deify departed spirits and advocate Polytheism? Do they not avow a purpose to war against present religious institutions and introduce a "*new theology?*" Do they not advertise their meetings as *religious meetings?* Were they not horrified when the Boston *Traveller* refused to publish their meetings with "Religious Notices," in February last? Do they not speak much more about spirits and spiritualism, than about Christ and Christianity? Do they not entreat the assistance of spirits? Do they not tell us that the spirits dispense mercies, and that wisdom, knowledge, strength and protection are obtained from them? Do they not tell of great illumination, exceeding joy and consolation derived from spiritual intercourse? Do they not declare that by the assistance and instruction thus received they are much better prepared to buffet the ills of life, and to meet death with sustaining hope, than they ever would have been under the instructions of the Bible? Yes, candid reader, all this is true. Why, then, is not our charge made good?

Let them not flatter themselves that they are not idolators because they do not bow down to spirits as the Christian does when he worships God. Idolatrous devotion was never a perfect counterfeit of true religion, nor celebrated with the same ceremonies as the Jewish or Christian worship. The worship of demons among the Greeks was very unlike Christian worship. Still they were worshipers, and were candid enough to acknowledge it. One of the Grecian philosophers said, that during a feast in honor of Bacchus, he had seen all Athens, men, women and children, drunk together. Says Dr. Hebbe: "The rites assumed a more passionate and furious character; exhibiting the utmost mental and physical excitement. The manifestations of this holy frenzy was strongest among the women, whose religious susceptibilities overstepped the bounds of reason and common decency. Crowds of them, clothed with fawn-skins, and bearing the sanctified thyrsus, flocked to the solitudes of Parnassus, or Cithæron, or Taygetus, during the consecrated triennial period, passed the night there with torches in one hand, dancing or rather running wildly about, screaming and shouting the name of the god, and sometimes divested of all clothing, their heads and loins encircled with vine-leaves, and indulging in the wildest antics, until they became giddy and fell in the most horrible delirium."

It is obvious from the testimony of prominent spiritualists that their devotional performances are "*often*" not less revolting than those of the Greeks!

JUDGE EDMONDS said, in the *Tabernacle* last spring: "We have to contend with our own fanaticism; for I assure you, from my own experience and observation, that the fascination of this intercourse is so great that its tendency is to lead the mind away from its proper judgment, and instill a spirit of fanaticism most revolting to the calm and natural mind."

"AMHERST," in No. 187 of the *Spiritual Telegraph*, gives us to understand that spiritualists "*grovel in the dirt, howl like wild beasts, and turn the meetings into perfect Pandemoniums. . . . We often see spiritual circles and meetings character-*

ized by such manifestations as the howlings, etc., above referred to. This *may* be worship, but it seems to me that the regards of a kind and loving Father are not likely to be attracted by rushing into his presence accompanied by harsh cymbals, Chinese-gongs, tom-toms, and other like melodious demonstrations. If there should be published in the columns of this paper, a record of the things transpiring at the regular meetings of a large proportion of the circles in our country, it would be considered a tissue of fables. It would be difficult for most persons—not participants—to believe that so much trash should be patiently listened to, and, especially, accredited to a spiritual source. *At some circles, the manifestations assume the most grotesque character, and so far as any one has been able to discover, without a rational use. The writer has seen mediums rolling on the floor, uttering grunts like swine ; giving vent to the most hideous yells ; and at times beatiny their bodies and tearing their hair like lunatics* !"

We have heard of many performances that have been enacted at the instigation of the spirits, which are too disgusting to be here described.

Christianity has its forms and institutions. Idolatry has its ceremonies and rites. They ever have been, and doubtless ever will be, different in many respects.

To be an idolator it is only necessary that a man should sustain the same relation to another being which ought to exist between himself and Jehovah. The spiritualists sustain this relation to the spirits. The Lord requires the will, confidence and service of man. The spirits demand this. He has given his people a rule of faith and practice; has promised them assistance and consolation in this life, and unending bliss in that which is to come. The spirits pretend to do the same.

The relation between the Lord and his people is compared in the Bible to that of marriage.* The spiritualists illustrate the relation between themselves and the spirits by the same comparison.

JOHN S. WILLIAMS, medium, of Cincinnati, Ohio, under oath before Mayor Westervelt, of this city, deposed, "I am not bound to my monitors otherwise than a good wife is bound to her husband, whom she sincerely believes more capable of conducting her through life, and is desirous of continually benefitting her; or, as a good husband to such a wife, setting aside all legal bonds; yet I try to *obey* my monitors."—*Synopsis, p.* 16.

Is it not obvious that the spirits usurp the prerogatives of God, and that those who follow them are idolators? The ancient pagans had images, and the moderns have *spent much time and money in attempting to make a divining image!* Their boasted "progression" is in fact a rapid retrogression towards heathenism.

* Jer. 3: 14—Eph. 7: 22, 23.

Perhaps they may be interested in hearing from their more benighted, but equally orthodox brethren in foreign lands.

In the "Youth's Day-Spring" for June, 1853, a missionary describing the alarm and grief of the Africans on the Gaboon river, at the near prospect of a death in their village, says: 'the room was filled with women, who were weeping in the most piteous manner, and calling on the *spirits of their fathers and of others who are dead*, and upon all spirits in whom they believe, Ologo, Njembi, Abambo, and Mbwini, to save the man from death. These spirits could not help them, but they knew of none mightier, and so called on them. Mr. White, a Wesleyan missionary, says: 'There is a class of people in New Zealand, called Eruku, or priests. These men pretend to have intercourse with departed spirits, . . by which they are able to kill by incantation any person on whom their anger may fall."*

"A recent English traveler gives an interesting account of the Yezidis, an Asiatic tribe, who 'serve the devil,' not in the sense implied by the phrase in Christian countries, but by actually worshiping the devil. The Mahomedan Beys, who cherish a most orthodox hatred of his brimstoneship, and always spit with great emphasis when his name is pronounced, have for many years waged an exterminating war against his disciples, burning them in

* Bliss on the Apocalypse, p. 260.

caves, crucifying them, and stocking their *serais* with the best looking of the female devil-worshipers; all for the glory of Allah and the Prophet. It appears that the Yezidis believe Satan to be the chief of the angelic host, now suffering in Tophet, for rebellion, but to return hereafter from transportation, and resume his high estate in the celestial hierarchy. On the principle that it is prudent to conciliate him in his misfortunes, in order to have a stronger claim upon him when he shall be restored to power, they sink at his offences, and in their daily prayers tender to him the assurance of their highest consideration. In the meantime, the Musselmens cut them up right and left; and the more they beseech the devil to help them, the more he never listens to them."

We have now shown that the gods of the ancient Pagans were the spirits of the dead, that Spiritualists deify and advocate the deification of dead men, that they invoke the assistance of departed spirits, and inculcate Polytheism.

We have shown that Spiritualists deny the existence of JEHOVAH, and contend that nothing but a council of departed spirits can be justly styled a Supreme Deity.

We have shown that necromancy results in *idolatry*, that the devotional exercises of some of the Spiritualists are as riotous as were those of the ancient Pagans; and that the boasted "progression" of the former, is but a progression in *Paganism*.

CHAPTER XII.

PRETENDED ANIMATION OF A DIVINING IMAGE.

"Thou shalt not make unto thee any graven image, or any likeness of anything that is in heaven above, or that is in the earth beneath, or that is in the water under the earth."—EXODUS XX: 4.

THE devotees of demons in this country, if we except a few Chinese, succeeded in dispensing with the use of *images* in their devotions and communion with their divinities for several years. But as the want of such an important and time-honored appendage to this anti-christian intercourse was deeply realized, and as ordinary patterns, such as are exhibited in the "Missionary Rooms" in Boston and New York, were unsuited to this "progressive age," in 1854, the spirits and their votaries applied their combined skill to supply the lamentable defect. The Spiritual brotherhood of Boston and vicinity, headed by John M. Spear, the Boston seer, at the instigation and under the direction of the spirits, constructed a complicated *divining image in the shape of a man,* at an expense of about two thousand dollars, and set it up—not on "the plains of Dura"—but on High Rock, Lynn, Mass.

The constructors of the image claimed that it was to be the embodiment of principles and forces in nature, which had never been understood till divulged by the spirits, and that it was to be *semi-human!* Mr. Hewett, of Boston, in giving its history in the *New Era* of June 21, 1854, says:

"The Electric Motor is an exact *correspondence* of the human body, at least, in so far as *involuntary motion* is concerned."

The strange mechanism of this image obviously originated not only in a desire on the part of the demons to gain notoriety and influence, but in a purpose to palm off on the world as an "*Electrical Motor*," a machine to be propelled, like Mr. Koons' "electrical table," *by themselves*, to represent it to be an *artificial wonder*, but the *result of natural laws*, and a complete counterpart to the "*miraculous conception*" of the Redeemer; in order to throw contempt on the Biblical account of his origin and destroy the belief that he was the *Son of God!*

Mr. Davis, the seer, says of the image, "There has been an attempt to infuse *human* vitality into the *mineral* substances, on the religious theory of the 'miraculous conception,' for which, however, the spirits have divulged what is considered a natural explanation."

Concerning this most scandalous "attempt" respecting the birth of a soul to this idol, the *New Era* says:

"There has been such an attempt on the part of the spirits, and that it has been successful, we have abundant evidence, in both the principle involved, and in the results which have since followed. Strange as it may seem, *neither* of the two distinct periods of motion arrived, till *after* a regular and ordinary arrangement of certain peculiar, mediumistic persons, in certain specific relations to the mechanism of human vitality or living aura had taken place.

"It was announced to Mrs. ———, by spiritual intelligences, several months since, that she should become a mother in some new sense—*that she should be the Mary of a New Dispensation.*

"Previously to this, Mrs. ———, had for some time experienced certain sensations analogous to those attendant upon gestation. Subsequently these indications gradually increased, until they at length became very marked and inexplicable, and presented some very singular characteristics. At length a request came, through the instrumentality of J. M. Spear, that on a certain day she should visit the tower at High Rock. None in the flesh—herself least of all—had any conception of the object of that visit. When there, however—suitable preparations having been carefully made by superior direction, though their purpose was incomprehensible—she began to experience the peculiar and agonizing sensations of parturition—differing somewhat from the ordinary experience, inasmuch as the throes were *internal* and of the *spirit*, rather than of the physical nature ; but nevertheless quite as uncontrollable and not less severe than those pertaining to the latter. This extraordinary physiological phenomenon continued for the space of about two hours. Its purpose and results were wholly incomprehensible to all but herself; but her own perceptions, clear and distinct, that in these agonizing throes, the most interior and refined elements of her spiritual being were imparted to, and absorbed by the appropriate portions of the mechanism—its minerals having been made peculiarly receptive by previous chemical processes.

" * * * * * The result of this phenomenon was that indications of life or pulsation, became apparent in the mechanism—first, to her own keenly sensitive touch, and soon after to the eyes of all beholders. These pulsations continued to increase, under a process which she was impelled to continue for some weeks, precisely analogous to that of nursing—for which preparation had previously been made in her own organism, while she was in utter ignorance of any such design—until at times a very marked and surprising motion resulted.

* * * * * * *

" Neither Mrs. ——— nor myself can profess to have, as yet, any definite conception as to what this 'new-born child'—the so-called 'Electrical Motor'

—is to be. However 'enthusiastic' or 'extravagant' may be the expectations of others, we do not know that we yet at all comprehend the ultimate designs of the intelligences engaged in it."—*New Era*, June 28, 1854.

So it appears that when the machinery of this complicated idol had been completed, it was found to be minus a *soul*—that Mrs. Somebody had spiritually conceived by the spirit of some dead man and had actually borne a soul to the image! and that she had been nursing the soul, or the *image*, we are not informed which, and that this offspring was likely to *live and grow!*

The most unbounded hopes were cherished and the most extravagant language was employed concerning this blasphemously styled "*Physical Saviour!*"

Says Mr. Hewett: "*The deep satisfaction which we enjoy, that the world is by and by to be blessed beyond conception, by this physical Saviour, through whose instrumentality, a permanent material basis shall be laid for true spiritual salvation, is beyond all price.*"

Says Mr. Capron: "Quite a number of persons, of great intelligence, candor, and unimpeachable character, fully believed in this second edition of the miraculous conception and birth, and the most unbounded enthusiasm was manifested by many. It was denominated the 'New Motive Power, Physical Saviour, Heaven's Last Best Gift to Man, New

Creation, The Great Spiritual Revelation of the Age, The Philosopher's Stone, the Art of all Arts, the Science of all Sciences,' and various other extravagant epithets were applied to this wonderful, new birth.

The machine itself was constructed at High Rock, Lynn, Mass. ; but several of the prominent *accouchers* were residents of Boston !"—*Modern Spiritualism, p.* 224.

As we are not informed who was the father of this child, we are naturally desirous to know what he will become, whether he will be a giant, and what will be his progeny, and their mighty works ! Fortunately we are not left in darkness on the subject.

"In the *New Era* of July 5th, we find a vision had by J. Wolcott, which developes what is expected to be accomplished by this machine. It appeared to grow in size, and 'threw off from itself smaller machines after its own pattern,' and those 'in turn threw off a multitude of other little ones.' Then he says :

"Next there appeared a movement among the machines ; and the larger ones, which were now fully developed, moved away over the plain into the distance. In their path stood a great number of churches, of every size and variety, from the diminutive Methodist Chapel, up to the stately Gothic Minster, and St. Paul's Cathedral. But the machines did not turn out of their course at all—running over and through those temples, completely demolishing them to heaps of worthless rubbish."

Thus it appears that this new race of beings, part wood, part steel, part loadstone, part demon, and part Mrs. Somebody, was to have been chiefly distinguished by a wholesale destruction of Meeting Houses! Probably this was out of a justifiable resentment, for rejection and neglect of the spirits, on the part of Christians! or, are the spirits determined to destroy all places of worship except those dedicated to themselves? This vision is certainly a very suggestive one.

But these sanguine devotees of demons reckoned in the absence of their host; they were destined to be disappointed; a slight defect was discovered in the divining image. *The spirits could not make it move to any purpose!*

Mr. Davis accounted for this on the ground that the whole thing was a mere *experiment* on the part of the spirits who were incompetent to perfect it. He says: 'That the progressive construction, *the private history*, so to speak, of this mechanism —the manner pursued, by which, from time to time, one part has been added after and to another—proves the whole work to be essentially experimental, conducted very honestly, and at friend Spear's expense, by several persons in the other world, who, doubtless, have the *correct philosophy* of the development of the New Motive

Power, and who are *deficient in the practical knowledge* of the means to consummate its actualization."

To this, Mr. Hewett of the *New Era*, replies: "We were very early informed that some things of a subordinate character about the motor, might, with propriety, be classed among the *experimentals*, but the *thing itself* was sure. From that moment among others, it became with us a *question of morals*, and is so still. Convince us that the main thing is an experiment, simply, and we shall be very far from thinking that even the *spirits*, who communicate under such circumstances, are *honest*. Our reasons are then: In the first place, they plainly told us, it was not an *experiment*. Now, if it were an experiment, they *falsified*, and that was *immoral*. In the second place, they had *no right*, though immortal, any more than mortals here, to involve our reputation and our pecuniary means in mere *experiment*, without telling us plainly that it was such. If it were an experiment, therefore, it was *dishonest*, in this second particular, as well as the first. But our whole experience in relation to this matter has been such as wholly and forever to preclude the idea of dishonest and experimenting spirits."

Why then does not the thing work? The ready answer of Mr. Hewett is:

"The revelation, as well as the motive power, is only in its incipient stages of development. *The child is born only*. It does not yet claim *to be a man.* Would it not be wiser to wait a little and witness its growth, than to attempt the strangulation of the infant? . . . . .

"Did he expect that as soon as the *child was born*, he would be able to perform the feat of Hercules, or fulfill the dream of Archimedes, and 'move the world?' If so, he shows but little appreciation of the philosophy of this matter. We repeat, that although the child is born, he does not claim to be a man."

But Mr. Hewett *was deceived,* notwithstanding his strong confidence in the morality and veracity of the demons. The whole affair proved to be an unsuccessful and most mortifying "*experiment*," and according to the logic of Mr. Hewett, the spirits "*falsified*" and were "*immoral.*" A large number of intelligent persons were sadly hoaxed, as they should ever expect to be, by these heathen divinities.

This wonderful child did not live! What became of its soul we are not informed; or whether its 'mother' dressed in mourning doth not appear.

Mr. Spear has written its

OBITUARY.

"It was moved, as you know, to Randolph, N. Y., that it might have the advantages of that lofty electrical position. A temporary building was erected to shelter it. Into that, under the cover of the night, the mob entered, tore out the heart of the mechanism, trampled beneath their feet, and scattered it to the four winds. I know the friends who were engaged in constructing this mechanism, and those who cheerfully gave of their means to promote the work, will mourn that the world has not yet arrived at a condition when it could welcome a philanthopic effort of this kind ; but thus it is. It did not wish the effort to succeed, and it determined it should not."

* * * *

"From the hour that the Electricizers expressed a desire to unfold to the inhabitants of this earth more perfectly a knowledge of electrical, magnetical, and ethereal laws that a new motive power might be exhibited, I said to them, 'Friends, my time, my strength, my means, my influence to aid a work so important and so beneficent are at your disposal.' Aided by several philanthropic and highly intelligent gentlemen, to whom their plan was unfolded and the model exhibited, labors were commenced, some two hundred highly scientific and very philosophic discourses were communicated : and at *precisely the time designated*, and at the point expected, *motion appeared, corresponding to embryotic life.*

"But the mob has done its work. The little mechanism has been assailed, torn asunder, and trampled beneath the feet of man."—*Telegraph, Oct.*, 1854.

Alas for the fate of the idol! Let not its devotees mourn as though some *strange* thing had happened.

A similar calamity befel one of its most noted predecessors by a more potent hand:

"And when they arose early on the morrow morning, behold, Dagon *was* fallen upon his face to the ground before the ark of the LORD; and the head of Dagon and both the palms of his hands *were* cut off upon the threshold; only *the stump of* Dagon was left to him." 1 Sam. 5: 4.

"And the idols He shall utterly abolish. And they shall go into the holes of the rocks, and into the caves of the earth, for fear of the LORD, and for the glory of his majesty, when he ariseth to shake terribly the earth." Isa. 2: 18, 19.

MESSIAH'S FUTURE REIGN.

From the sublime Prize Poem of

REGINALD HEBER, BISHOP OF CALCUTTA.

" And who is He ! the vast, the awful form,
Girt with the whirlwind, sandal'd with the storm ?
A western cloud around his limbs is spread,
His crown a rainbow, and a sun his head.
To highest heaven he lifts his kingly hand,
And treads at once the ocean and the land ;
And hark ! his voice amidst the thunder's roar,
His dreadful voice, that time shall be no more !
Lo ! cherub hands the golden courts prepare,
Lo ! thrones are set, and every saint is there ;
Earth's utmost bounds confess his awful sway,
The mountain's worship, and the isles obey :
Nor sun, nor moon they need—nor day—nor night ;—
God is their temple and the Lamb their light ;
And shall not Israel's sons exulting come,
Hail the glad beam and claim their ancient home ?
On David's throne shall David's offspring reign,
And the dry bones be warm with life again.
Hark ! white rob'd crowds their deep hosannahs raise,
And the hoarse flood repeats the sound of praise ;
Ten thousand harps attune the mystic song,
Ten thousand thousand saints the strain prolong !
'Worthy the Lamb ! omnipotent to save,
'Who died, who lives triumphant o'er the grave.' "

INCREDULITY OF THOMAS. CHRIST RESURRECTED.

"BEHOLD MY HANDS AND MY FEET, THAT IT IS I MYSELF: HANDLE ME AND SEE; FOR A SPIRIT HATH NOT FLESH AND BONES, AS YE SEE ME HAVE."—Luke xxiv. 39. *See page* 194.

CHAPTER XIII.

CREED OF THE SPIRITUALISTS.

"Though we, or an angel from heaven, preach any other gospel unto you than that which we have preached unto you, let him be accursed."—GALATIANS i: 8.

THE spiritualists pretend that they have no creed. Creed is from the Latin *Credo*, which signifies belief; and each and every one of them has his belief or creed. It matters little whether their creed be written or oral; each has his own creed in his mind, which may be sufficient for his purposes.

Several important reasons militate against the formal publication of the articles which they now hold in common.

It would be difficult to trace the orbit of a wandering star.

In their downward course from bad to worse, their degeneracy will be less apparent and startling if their position is undefined and their creed is unpublished. Their faith and works are much better adapted to darkness than light. The demons can be seen and work better in a dark room than in the light, and their doctrines appear to better advantage in darkness.

Their system of theology and ethics is not sufficiently matured to be trusted to commend and defend itself. Like their image, it is only a "babe" yet.

It would be bad policy frankly to publish their sentiments to the world before they occupy a stronger position, and ensnare some thousands more in their toils. If they were too fast in publishing their sentiments, they might be overthrown.

While Christians, whose faith is sustained by the word of God, frankly proclaim their belief to the world, these by the pretence that they are exceeding liberal and charitable, and to apologize for the non-publication of their most offensive views, boast that they have *no creed.*

They have a creed and system of theology which may be very appropriately denominated *The doctrines of demons.** They are very confident that their views are correct.

Says Mr. Capron: "Their general theology is that of Davis, Swedenborg and others, who have claimed to receive their impressions from the spirits." We know of those who think the theological teaching wrong, but that cannot be proved."†

Mr. Fishbough informed the writer, that their doctrines were substantially the same with those of A. J. Davis.

* 1 Tim. 4: 1. † Singular Revelations, p. 65.

Mr. BRITTAN says: "It is readily granted that spiritualism rejects the common notions respecting 'a fall of angels,' 'total depravity,' and the atonement." "We do reject the resurrection as taught by the accredited authorities in *mythological theology*,"* meaning Christianity.

Mr. A. E. NEWTON, of Boston, styles the Biblical doctrine of the Resurrection of the body, a "*crude contradictory and impossible speculation*."†

SPIRITUALISM OPPOSED TO THE BIBLE.

CREED OF THE SPIRITUALISTS. "ANOTHER GOSPEL."	TESTIMONY OF THE BIBLE. THE TRUTH.
I. We believe it to be right and highly beneficial to hold intercourse with departed spirits, and to covenant with them to remain with us as our familiar friends and guardians.	Should not a people seek unto their God? The soul that turneth after such as have familiar spirits, and after wizards, I will even set my face against that soul, and will cut him off from among his people.
II. We believe the Hebrew prophets were inspired by the spirits of the dead, just as mediums are inspired in these days.	The prophecy came not in old time by the will of man; but holy men of God spake as they were moved by the Holy Ghost.
III. We believe that all of the human race will finally be saved.	Strait is the gate, and narrow is the way, which leadeth unto life, and few they be that find it.

* Review of Beecher, p. 45. † Letter to the Edward's Church, p. 21.

IV. We believe that Jesus Christ is the Son of God as much as any other man, and no more. He was not begotten by the Holy Spirit.	The angel answered and said unto her, the Holy Ghost shall come upon thee, and the power of the Highest shall overshadow thee: therefore also that holy thing which shall be born of thee shall be called the Son of God.
V. We do not believe that Christ atoned for the sins of the world.	He hath made him to be a propitiation for our sins, and not for ours only, but for the sins of the whole world.
VI. We do not believe in the fall of angels.	The angels which kept not their first estate, he has reserved in everlasting chains under darkness unto the Judgment of the great day.
VII. We believe the resurrection takes place at death.	I will raise him up at the *last day.*
VIII. We believe that Christ's body was never raised from the tomb.	Behold my hands and my feet, that it is I myself: handle me, and see; for a spirit hath not *flesh and bones, as ye see me have.*
IX. We believe that God will never raise the bodies of the dead from their graves.	The hour is coming, in the which all that are in the graves shall hear his voice, and shall come forth; they that have done good unto the resurrection of life; and they that have done evil unto the resurrection of damnation. *

* The word Resurrection, occurs 39 times in the New Testament. It is from the Greek *Anastasis,* which signifies *standing up.* Nothing short of the *resurrection of the body* will meet its signification.

X. We believe the Judgment is going on constantly. There is no special day for adjudication and rewards.

He hath appointed a day in the which he will judge the world. Who shall judge the quick and the dead at his appearing and his kingdom.

THE ASCENSION OF CHRIST.

XI. We believe that Christ will never personally appear on earth again.

This same Jesus, which is taken up from you into heaven, shall so come in like manner as ye have seen him go into heaven. Behold he cometh with clouds and every eye shall see him.

XII. We believe that the spiritual developments of the present time are foretold in the Scriptures as the second coming of Christ.

Then if any man shall say unto you, Lo, here is Christ, or there; believe it not. For there shall arise false Christs; and false prophets. If they say he is in the desert go not forth: behold, he is in the secret chambers, believe it not.

XIII. We believe that the miracles of the Spiritualists are of the same character and wrought by the same agencies with those of Christ and the Apostles.	And they shall show great signs and wonders; insomuch that if it were possible, they shall deceive the very elect. After the working of satan with all power and signs and lying wonders, and with all the deceivableness of unrighteousness in them that perish.
XIV. We believe the Scriptures to be "the paper and ink relics of Christianity, a foundation as impermanent as the changeful sand." *	All Scripture is given by inspiration of God.
XV. We believe that the spirits will communicate universally, that the most of mankind will be obliged to heed them, which will bring the FINAL CRISIS!	Now the Spirit speaketh expressly, that in the latter times some shall depart from the faith, giving heed to seducing spirits, and doctrines of devils.
XVI. We believe that with the aid of the spirits we shall wage a successful warfare against Christianity as it now exists; against the religious sects; and against the Bible as they understand it. By our astounding miracles people will be constrained to believe.	We wrestle not against flesh and blood, but against principalities, against powers, against the rulers of the darkness of this world, against spiritual wickedness in high places; or "*wicked spirits*," in "heavenly places," as the *margin* reads.
XVII. We believe that Spiritualism will introduce the Millennium. Then all can hold intercourse with spirits.	Though we, or an angel from heaven, preach any other gospel unto you than that which we have preached unto you, let him be accursed.

* Davis' Review of Bushnell, pp. 21, 24.

CHAPTER XIV.

THE EVILS OF SPIRITUALISM.

"Manasseh . . . used enchantments, and used witchcraft, and dealt with a familiar spirit, and with wizards: he wrought much evil in the sight of the LORD to provoke him to anger."—2 CHRON. xxxiii: 6.

"IF there is anything intrinsically wrong in the course we incline to pursue, or necessarily injurious in the intercourse itself, we desire to know in what that wrong or injury is made to consist."—*Brittan's Review of Beecher*, p. 26.

"We challenge you, as men—as earnest men, as men desiring the good of your fellows—to come forth and meet us in the fight, expose our errors, draw the shroud away, and enable the world to see us as we are. We challenge you to come and do that thing."—*Address of the Society for the Diffusion of Spiritual Knowledge.*

We have already shown that spiritualism is essentially the same with the necromancy and sorcery forbidden in the Scriptures. Whatever God has prohibited *must be "intrinsically wrong."*

It must be wrong to heed the spirits, because *in*

so doing every person is liable to be grossly deceived. Messrs. Spear and Hewett, of Boston, with their associates, were lamentably victimized in the matter of the divining image. The demons assured them that they were not experimenting, and that when the image was completed they would surely invest it with life, so that it would speak. According to Mr. Hewett, the constructors of the image acted on the presumption that the spirits would not falsify and would not commit any moral wrong. But when, at an expense of about 2,000 dollars, the image was completed, it turned out that the whole thing was an "*experiment*," the spirits "*falsified*" and their confidants were "*deceived!*" But, strange to say, this was not enough. As though to prove for once that

"A little learning is a dangerous thing,"

Mr. Spear was prepared to take another lesson of a similar character and be duped again.

A correspondent of the Boston Investigator, writing from Randolph last winter, says:

"The spiritualists here, under the guidance of Rev. John M. Spear, don't despair of success in something. They are now spending $80 per week digging a hole in the ground for the discovery of the fossil remains of an ancient race of beings that lived 18,000 years ago!—The most elevated and reliable class of spirits have informed Mr. Spear, that the above race was wealthy, that they made it a business to accumulate property, and their wealth was buried with them, the nature of which has not been disclosed—whether gold, silver, or precious stones, remains to be ascertained. One of our most respectable citizens, a man of wealth and integrity, is now engaged in this business, and is following the directions of the spirits in every respect!"

Spiritualistic Bigamy.

"A singular case of bigamy recently occurred in this city, which illustrates the new uses to which spiritual raps may be appropriated. A woman named Susan A. Hubbard was arrested for the above offence, and taken before Judge Osborne, of the Lower Police Court, for a hearing, on the 20th inst. It was alleged that she had three or four husbands; but it was necessary only to prove the existence of two marriages. Rev. Mr. Saggart, a Baptist clergyman, one of the witnesses, identified the prisoner as the person whom he had, some years since, married to Hubbard. Hubbard himself was present, and was also identified by the witness—thus proving that he was not dead, but had unfortunately 'turned up.'

"The second husband (or rather one of the subsequent husbands) was also present, and swore to his recent marriage with the defendant. Mr. Smucker, the counsel for the prosecution, wished to know the circumstances under which the last marriage had been brought about. The witness, Henry

W. Smith, was a school-master. He had first met the prisoner at an assemblage of spiritualists, on the corner of Broadway and Lispenard street. She was a prominent member of the circle, which met there from time to time, to summon the world of spirits to their presence and interrogate them. The prisoner gradually became acquainted with the witness, (a robust, good-looking young man,) and having conceived a passion for him, set about the work of inducing him to marry her. He heard that she had former husbands, and wished to know if they were dead. At the next meeting she summoned the whole of them from the land of shadows, and made them all, one after the other, testify to the fact that they were dead, (in the body,) and give other interesting items as to their spiritual condition. The young man, being a firm believer in spiritualism, could not, of course, deny such evidence ; and being attracted by the smartness, intelligence and good looks of the 'medium,' he married her. Not long after, he discovered that her 'spiritual manifestations' were lying manifestations, and that there were three or four other claimants to the possession of his wife, one of whom was *black!*"—*New York paper.*

A Family Ruined by Spiritualism.

Mr. George Doughty, a respectable farmer of Flushing, Long Island, "possessed of considerable property, having his interest excited by the reports of the doings of the mediums of this mischievous and absurd delusion, resolved to seek out one of the professors of the spiritual doctrines, and make himself acquainted with the mysteries which they pretend to disclose. With that intention he proceeded to the city of Pittsburgh, Pennsylvania, where he was introduced to a professed medium, a lady named Mrs. French, whom, after a short acquaintance, he invited to visit him and his family on Long Island; and from that time—some two years ago—up to within a recent date, she has been a constant visitor at the farmer's house, where she was, at the wish of the unfortunate man, treated as one of the family.

"A few weeks since, however, she arrived in the city of New York, and instead of proceeding direct to the farmer's, as she was wont to do, took rooms at the Irving House, where she was accompanied by a strange man, whom, she informed the farmer upon visiting her, was about writing an interesting legend of the spirit land, she furnishing the materials and the matter. Such was the influence she had acquired over the farmer, and the strange delusion under which he labored, that she induced him to adopt her as his daughter, and finally to make over to her nearly his entire property.

"The wife of the unfortunate victim endeavored to restrain him in his mad career, but did not succeed. By threats of violence, he compelled his gentle partner to make an assignment of her interest in his affairs to him; after which, he proceeded to convert his effects into cash—which amounted to about 15,000 dollars in all—and this he immediately paid over to the medium at the Irving House, upon which the latter took *French*-leave and departed, going, it is reported, back to Pittsburgh. The next day he seemed partly to realize the extent of his folly, and called upon his friend the medium—but lo, and behold! the charming creature was missing, as was also the fabulous book-writer. He then asked to be shown to the room she had occupied, and declared he would commit suicide. His request was of course refused, and he was driven from the house. He then proceeded to the residence of an acquaintance in New York, and there repeated his determination to shuffle off this mortal coil. He finally went home, and his friends, with very natural misgivings as to the propriety of permitting him to have unlimited liberty, had him arrested and conveyed to the New York Lunatic Asylum, where he now remains a confirmed lunatic. * * * The victim of the conspiracy is the father of two very interesting daughters, and has many respectable relatives and connexions in this city, whose feelings with regard to the sad event may be easily imagined. Such are the particulars of one of the most infamous cases of heartless fraud and delusion which has probably ever been recorded. The reputed medium is reported to be an abandoned female of the worst character."—*Brooklgn Daily Eagle, Feb.* 25, 1852.

Since the family of poor Doughty were thus left to grieve in comparative poverty, the successful medium has occasionally made her appearance in New York. She sometimes rides in a splendid carriage, and parades herself "dressed in the richest crimson silk, and loaded with heavy gold ornaments, chains, bracelets, rings, etc., etc."*

Encouraged by her unparalleled success, she continues to officiate in the capacity of a *medium*. At the present time a *Mrs. French, from Pittsburgh*, occupies a room next door to the private sanctum of the Editor of the *Spiritual Telegraph!*

He honors her with the following notice:

"Mrs. E. J. French, clairvoyant physician, has taken an office in our establishment, 342 Broadway, where she proposes to hold her *seances* for the investigation and treatment of diseases, etc., and where she will be happy to meet all who may be in need of her services."

And why should she not occupy the chair of Chief Medium at Head Quarters? We were informed by a gentleman engaged in the "establishment," that she was a *superior medium!*—the veritable Mrs. French from Pittsburgh,—and doubtless the same by whom Mr. Doughty was bewitched and ruined. Certainly her works and her eminent success entitle her to a distinguished position in this

* Spirit-Rapping Unveiled, p. 236.

"New Dispensation," as A. J. Davis styles this anti-christian delusion.

JUDGE EDMONDS' remarks in the *Telegraph* concerning a letter from San Francisco, by which he was deceived,—"If the object was to show me the *dangers of spiritual intercourse, and how liable we are to be deceived by false or fabricated communications, it was quite unnecessary, for I long ago learned that*, and have earnestly, once and again, given utterance to a warning against that danger."

The following heart-rending cases were published in the *N. Y. Medical Gazette :*

"A case of insanity has occurred within a few days, by reason of the revelation made by mysterious raps, that the steamship Atlantic had been wrecked with the loss of all on board ; although since this melancholy catastrophe, the passengers, whose 'spirits' were declared to have made the rapping, have arrived at home—one of them to find his wife a maniac, from a belief in these ghostly knockings. Another female has just been sent to the asylum, by reason of the mesmeric operations upon her nervous system, avowedly for the purpose of rendering her clairvoyant, but with the effect of dooming her to lunacy. And these recent instances are not merely isolated cases, for in several of the asylums, the victims of these kindred impostures, are hopelessly insane."

This Intercourse is Injurious to Health.

Spiritualists testify that it is very injurious to invalids, to sit in their circles; and that intercourse with spirits is very exhausting to mediums, who frequently spend sleepless nights in consequence. Mr. Sunderland said he had lost ten pounds of flesh in two months by this intercourse.

Spiritualism, like mesmerism, its forerunner, is dementing to the mind and injurious to the body.

Mr. Brittan says: "If it be a fact that *spirits whose influence is unfavorable to the health and happiness of the medium, do sometimes influence men in the body, as Mr. Beecher has most clearly shown*, it may be proper to dissipate that influence by such modes as shall prove to be most successful."*

The "most successful" way to "dissipate" drunkenness, is to abstain from all that intoxicates. Doubtless total abstinence from necromancy would be the best mode of averting its evils. Mr. Brittan confesses that the spirits sometimes ruin the health and happiness of the medium, but he can discover *nothing "wrong" or "injurious." in this intercourse.!*

Spirits Require the Will.

The Spirits require their mediums to yield themselves and their wills entirely to their control. "in

* Review of Beecher, p. 25.

order to prepare a medium, the person must give up all self-control, all resistence, and resign him or herself to the entire discretion and control of the spirits. Sometimes the process of preparation or developement is easy and quick, at other times it is protracted and difficult; but it is always rendered more easy and quicker of accomplishment, by perfect resignation and entire non-resistence."—*Philadelphia History of Spiritualism, p.* 11.

This is what none but God has a right to require. He has given us a *will* as a barrier against evil influences and temptations. Without it a man can scarcely say his soul is his own, not having so much the control of himself as the debased drunkard, he is like a city broken down and without walls, or a dismantled vessel at sea without a rudder.

We cannot "serve two masters." We cannot yield our wills to two beings. If we submit to God we cannot yield to the Spirits. Whoever obeys the latter sins against the former, The Spirits require a *service* also, to which they have no right.

"Many a friend has been estranged from those near to his heart, because he yielded up the dictates of his common sense to run wild after some *ignis-fatuus* of a real or supposititious Spirit-command. Does it seem right that a man should not only waste his precious hours, but be continually subjected to an overpowering influence that is silently but surely sapping his self-reliance, and preparing him for an existence without a purpose ?" —*Spiritual Telegraph, No* 182.

Spiritualism is Very Fascinating.

When once a person is brought under its influence, it is difficult to escape. Every form of evil has its enticements, but the seductive influence of necromancy is seldom equalled. Hundreds, by taking the first step, have been unwittingly drawn along till all their efforts to escape were futile.

A physician in Philadelphia, stated some time since, that he would have nothing more to do with spiritualism, but that it was *not in his power to extricate himself from the influence of the Spirits.*

Rev. Mr. Hobbs says he become a medium, and he was at times "*powerless in a terrible grasp!*"

The spirits are very anxious to subject people to their control. An intimate friend of ours living in New Jersey, indulged in a varied and ample experience, several years since, to satisfy himself of the character of these intelligences. In some instances they would discourse morality and religion marvellously; but when cross-examined they would become angry, dash the medium's hand along at a terrible rate, contradict themselves and swear most bitterly. Once they begged him to consent that the Lord should submit him to their charge. They were very anxious to become his guardians, but he recollected the afflicted Gadarene and the fate of the swine, and declined their proposals.

On another occasion ten of them, as they said, undertook to subject him by *force* to their servitude; but they were unequal to the task, though, as he declared, they produced an awful skull-splitting sensation! Once they tried to intimidate him by threats, when he defied them all. "Can't we hurt you?" said one. "Can you?" "*Can't we?*" "Can you?" "*Can't we?*" "In the name of the Lord, can you hurt any one?" "*If the Lord wills,*" answered the demons.

I have been informed by good authority that a woman in Philadelphia was magnetized, when the spirits took possession of her and kept her in that condition for two days and nights, in spite of all efforts to the contrary. The magnetiser watched her till the middle of the second night, when, realizing the want of sleep, he tied her in a large armchair so strongly that he supposed she could not extricate herself, and went to bed. He had slept but a short time, when he was awakened to find her, to his astonishment, entirely clear from chair and bands, and in the act of leaping out of a high window! He seized her just in time to save her life; when she exclaimed, "O, Dr. ——, I am not to blame, *the spirits made me do it!*"

Dr. Dexter gives us the following account in his Introduction to *Spiritualism*. It will serve to illustrate the conduct of the spirits when they exert their power:

"It was not till after I had become a writing medium, *against my will and determined efforts to the contrary*, that I yielded an implicit faith in the truth of spiritual intercourse with men. After the concerted and continued attempt to impress me had passed over, I refrained from visiting circles, and thought, by staying away, I might be free from any impression. On the contrary, my own arm would be moved while I was asleep, and awake me by its motion.

"During the time I abstained from sitting in any circle, *I was twice lifted bodily from my bed, moved off its edge, and thus suspended in the air!* * * * Heretofore my arm had been the organ to which their efforts had been chiefly directed; now, my whole body was subjected to their influence, *against my will and desire, and all my struggles to resist them.* * * * *

"Often when I am alone in my office, my hand will be moved, and I am obliged to abandon every other purpose till the spirits have concluded their communication. An incident of this kind happened some months since. After I had retired to bed, I was awakened from sleep by the rapid and violent motion of my hand. It was midnight. I could assign no cause for this manifestation, and essayed to throw off the influence, by all possible means, but in vain.

"I was compelled to rise, procure pencil and paper, and a long communication was written before they would again permit me to sleep."

From his own account it seems the Doctor became a servant of the spirits *against his will and determined efforts to the contrary!*—a mere machine "compelled to do their bidding or be tormented and spend sleepless nights!"

If we would be saved from the evils of necromancy we should "let it alone before it is meddled with." Said the Rev. Baptist Noel, "May God save us by his grace; but if ever we are saved we must shun the *beginnings* of evil."

SPIRITUALISM IS AN OBSTACLE TO THE CONVERSION OF THE SOUL.

Spirits impress the minds of mediums and those susceptible to their influence, and thus array them against Christ and the Bible. This is the natural tendency of Spiritualism. It would probably be very difficult to find a person who had become developed as a medium, or clairvoyant, who has since been converted to Christ. Every person feels that he has as much opposition as he can overcome to believe in Christ, apart from the influence of Spiritualism. He needs the full power of an unbiased mind, so that he can say in truth, like one of old, *I "will serve the Lord."* But Spiritualism deprives a man of this power, and places him in subjection to evil spirits.

If we esteem Christianity as a blessing, and the privileges which we enjoy in consequence of its dissemination, as preferable to those of heathen lands, we must deem Spiritualism, which wars against it, a great evil.

SPIRITUALISM IS FILLING OUR LAND WITH DEMONIACS.

Medium training is analogous to the work of breaking down the walls of a city. When once the wall is destroyed, the city may be entered by any enemy. So when a person has become a medium, he can be possessed and controlled by any prowling demon who chooses to do this.

The fully developed medium, who is entirely subjected to the control of the spirits, is but a passive automaton for the operation of demons, and just as really a *demoniac* as the victim represented in our first engraving.

MRS. CAUGHEY, a venerable Christian lady of this city, informed the writer that she had seen an amiable lady of twenty summers possessed by an evil spirit, thrust on to a couch, raging and frothing at the mouth, with glaring eyes, and agonizing contortions, cursing and praying almost in the same breath. The demon even cursed Jehovah, and swore by all that was vile and sacred that he would kill the medium!

Reader, think of a girl of fourteen summers, modest and mild, who, in consequence of becoming a medium, is possessed by an evil spirit, and with the ferocity of the furies, flies at the object of demoniac malice.

Imagine a medium of middle age, a lady generally mild, sitting in a "circle" with others, who instantly becomes furious—kicks over the table and chairs, and with book, footstool, or any missile assails one of the company.

Think of another of forty years, who is dashed upon the floor in spasms, possessed by a spirit who professed to have been a drunkard, who drank to drown trouble, and who declared that language was inadequate to describe his misery!

Imagine a man of twenty-five years, acting the drunkard, reeling, hurling chairs, playing the simpleton, and by turns becoming stupid, gloomy, angry, furious, for six hours together; and when at last freed from his tormentors, completely exhausted and unconscious of all that had passed.

These are not mere fancy pictures; they are drawn from life, and represent a large class of mediums in this city and elsewhere, whose names are screened from the public eye, out of regard to their feelings, their welfare, and the wishes of their friends.

The four cases last portrayed were minutely described to the writer by a *Spiritualist* of known veracity, as cases of which he was an eye witness!

He stated that *demoniacs were very numerous in this city and vicinity—much more so than spiritualists generally were willing to admit*—that he had seen many, and desired never to witness another.

This gentleman was Mr. William Fishbough, long known as an editor of spiritual publications.

JUDGE EDMONDS relates "that an evil spirit visited one of his circles, took possession of Mrs. S., the medium—manifested a very unhappy frame of mind, sometimes setting the company at defiance and acting as though he hated them. The medium was very much distressed by the whole thing, frequently wept bitterly, and resisted as far as she was able; but he seemed to have obtained entire possession of her, *compelling* her to do and to say things which she would gladly have avoided." After occupying their attention for most of the evening, "he left her, *but not until he had thrown her upon the floor in great distress.*"—*Spiritualism, p.* 464.

"AMHERST" says in *Telegraph No.* 182, he "has seen *mediums rolling on the floor, uttering grunts like swine; giving vent to the most hideous yells; and at times beating their bodies and tearing their hair like lunatics.* If we are doomed to see a beautiful faith disfigured with such manifestations as we sometimes now receive, let us *pray that there may be some one raised up amongst us who shall be endowed with power to cast out the 'unclean spirits.'*"

No wonder that they are apprehensive that their "beautiful faith" will be "*disfigured*"! If demoniacs are so numerous now, what may we not expect a few years hence, with such a host of "developing mediums" as are scattered all over the country?

The writer is acquainted with a young woman in New Hampshire, who has been occasionally possessed by a demon for several years. Her sufferings have been very great. She has barely escaped death many times. She must talk when others sleep and be wearied to death's door by innumerable tossings to and fro, till she is a mere wreck in body and mind; and death must soon end the painful scene.

A Biting Medium.

Chillicothe, Ohio, May 22, 1855.

S. W. Smith, *Dear Sir* :—I have recently visited the somewhat noted "*Biting Medium,*" in Scioto county, some fourteen miles west from Portsmouth. * * * The medium is a small boy with fair complexion, light hair, and blue eyes. The little fellow is evidently afraid of the strange order of intelligences that operate through him, as it required some persuasion on my part to obtain his consent to sit, in his usual manner, for the manifestations. He had to be invariably enveloped in a sheet or something of the kind, before the manifestations could be obtained. * * * The singular manifestations were rather more conclusive, than pleasant evidences of an unseen intelligence, as the evidence of the deep prints of teeth upon the bodies of divers persons, has pointedly testified. Some have been bitten till the blood trickled from the wound. Even the boy himself, escaped not the munchings of this toothful mouth. Pocket knives were taken from the hands of persons by the unseen agency, and their blades wrenched from their handles. Writing was performed under the cover of the sheet surrounding the boy; likewise musical instruments played upon. The Bible has been held before him, and its leaves turned and certain chapters pointed out, in the nothingness of air, unsupported by any visible power. Persons have retired to bed with the boy with the intention of sleeping with him through the night, but their intention was frustrated, they slept not, they were so harassed and bitten, they had to arise and seek repose in some other quarter. The little medium lives in a neighborhood where old madam 'awfuldoxy,'—Orthodoxy—bears the sway with her preposterous fables.—*Spiritual Universe.*

A Counterfeiting Demon.

'Some eight or nine months ago a well-known gentleman of this city, and an intimate friend of the writer, passed into the spirit-world. For several years previous to his death he had been a spiritualist, and during the latter portion of that time had been a medium. Previous and immediately subsequent to the interment of his body, he manifested his spirit-presence in a remarkable manner to different individuals, and especially to his widow, the latter being controlled to speak his words, and in one or two instances seeing him, apparently with the external eye, and as plainly as she had ever seen him in the flesh. * * * * While each of these were mourning the loss of two lovely children, the spirit of the gentleman aforesaid took possession of his wife's sister and kept her under his control continually for six days. During this time the medium was kept upon her bed, and the spirit re-enacted, through her, in the most perfect manner, the scenes of his last sickness, which was consumption. All the little peculiarities of those scenes, many of which were totally unknown to the medium, were minutely reproduced. There were the same short and labored breathing, the same hacking and expectorating cough, the same motions, gesticulations, exclamations, expressions of desire and aversion, that had been witnessed in the dying man; and what was still more convincing, he repeated, through the medium, conversations which had passed only between him and his wife, and alluded to facts known only to himself and her. This scene, be it remembered, was continued for six consecutive days, during which time the wife was scarcely permitted to leave the bedside. A more powerful test of identity could scarcely be conceived."—*Telegraph*, March 3, 1855.

How exquisitely delectable must have been this experience! All to prove what it did not prove!

Reader, if a spirit should carry you through such racking, coughing, and agonizing contortions, for six days and nights together, could you believe it to be the work of a relative or a friend? Just as though no other spirit could know enough of the man's last sickness to imitate his sufferings! And this is published as one of their "most powerful tests of identity"! Much more *powerful* than wise or merciful.

A Demoniac Loses Employment by "Good Spirits."

The following was written by the editor of the Mount Holly, *New Jersey Mirror*, and copied from that paper into the *Telegraph* of May 12, 1855:

"A servant girl living in the family of Sheriff Ivins, at Tom's River, Ocean County, not long since commenced acting so strangely as to excite the attention of every one who saw her. She was questioned in regard to her conduct, when she said she was under the control of some supernatural or spiritual agency, but could not in any way account for it—and that the spirits influencing her assured her they were *good spirits*. They would come and go at pleasure, leaving her to wonder at the sudden transformation in her feelings. While under the influence alluded to, her strength seemed almost equal to Samson's, and there was nothing about the house but what she could move without the least difficulty. She would pick up a barrel of flour, and with the greatest ease carry it up stairs. On one occasion she had got about half way up the steps with a barrel when the spirits left her, and with them her strength vanished, leaving her in a quandary, from which she was only relieved by several persons assisting in taking the flour down stairs. She would place her hand upon a table and tell it to travel, when it would move around the room and out of doors, and no power, save her own will, could stop it. And at one time four strong men attempted to hold the table to the floor, but they had no more effect upon it than so many infants.

"The Dutchmen in the neighborhood, when they conversed in their own language, would be told by her what they had said, which satisfied them that she was leagued with the devil. One day Mrs. Ivins visited a neighbor, and, on her return, the girl related the conversation that had taken place, and even told this lady her own thoughts in reference to discharging her—thoughts that Mrs. Ivins had never breathed to any one. Upon being asked how she knew this, she said the spirits had communicated it to her. She is entirely destitute of education, but frequently, when the spirits took possession of her, she would go up to her room and write, in a fair, legible hand, what they had dictated.

"The family at last became afraid of her, and notwithstanding she was the best girl for work they ever had, and her unwillingness to leave, it was found necessary to *discharge her, and she reluctantly departed to her father's residence*, at Bergen Iron Works. We have had positive assurances of the truth of these statements, direct from the family."

A CLERGYMAN BECOMES A DEMONIAC.

THE REV. B. S. HOBBS, of Little Falls, N. Y., thus writes on May 15, 1855, to the *Spiritual Telegraph* :

"It is now about four years since I professed faith in the doctrine that spirits can and do hold intercourse with man. Then, for a season, I had little doubt of its importance and its truth. But it was not mine to profess and cherish this then to me most precious faith, except for a short time, without literally falling a martyr to its profession! I was then regarded by some as a medium ; and thus I verily believed myself to be, as I exhibited the various phenomena common to, I was about to say, that unfortunate class. But of that time, and its consequent results, I wish not now to speak further than to say, that till that period *I had never known sorrow and suffering* in comparison to what I then was, most strangely indeed, compelled to endure. * * * * While on a visit to a distant part of the State from where I reside, I was called on by a friend to officiate at the funeral of a departed neighbor. I had, as usual, went through the introductory services, and commenced discoursing from my text, when, to my utter horror and mortification, *my mouth was suddenly closed, and for a time I could not utter a word.* Judge, reader, of my consternation and surprise, when the influence of former times returned upon me with redoubled fury, and I was again *powerless, in a terrible grasp,* from which I in vain sought for release ; and to add to my consternation, I was compelled, in spite of all my efforts, to speak the words, '*Spirits have power on the earth.*' Oh, reader ! *that* day to the writer of these lines, was a painful one indeed. That strange power did not release its hold until I *had acted in several* places in the capacity of a Spirit-medium, being, so far as I know, regarded as an undoubted one of that class. * * * Since that period until a few weeks past, I have not even made the attempt to speak again in public. But on the first Sabbath in the present month, I again made the attempt and succeeded. The following Sabbath I attempted to speak again, and now, reader, listen to the result ! *My mouth was again closed,* and not opened until I was thrown into the same state as mentioned before, and then and there was I compelled to deliver an address to the audience, professing to come from the spheres. I had another appointment at another place for the following Sabbath, but it is now withdrawn, and I here freely confess that I have no desire to make the attempt to preach another sermon, if I cannot do so without passing the ordeal I did on that occasion.

"I come now to the main object of this letter, which is to ask, Is what I have experienced Spirit-control ? and if so, why should my mouth be closed while endeavoring to preach the Gospel to my fellow-men ? Again, admitting this to be the fact, ought

I to submit to such control as this, in so far as I have the strength to resist its severe and strange power? The truth is, I have little fellowship for much that I have seen, called Spirit-influence. It is of a *strange* character, indeed! It is to me even *more* than strange that spirits of the spheres *can* do the work many now believe come from heaven.

"One thing is to me rationally clear—that much, *very* much that comes through that supposed channel, is *scarcely worthy of the imperfection of earth; and of the little I have seen there is still less that bears to me the evidence and the impress of truth.*"

So much for dabbling with the spirits! Mr. Hobbs should not think it strange that the demons closed his mouth when he was preaching. It is their chief business to oppose Christianity.

Demoniac Murders and Suicides.

Matthew Langdon, a printer in this city, 38 years of age, followed up the circles and consulted the spirits, out of anxiety to become a *seeing medium*, till he was instigated to cut his throat, which ultimately caused his death!

Dr. Elliot, surgeon at the Bellevue Hospital, to which Mr. Langdon was sent after his throat was cut, testified: "He told us he had been influenced by spiritual manifestations to commit suicide."—*N. Y. Times, Jan.* 8, 1853.

Two girls in Lawrence, Mass., a few years since, one the daughter of Mr. Ramsdell, a medium, believed the lie which the spirits then taught, that all were happier after death, and determined to commit suicide. When purchasing laudanum for this purpose, the druggist inquired what they wished it for, they replied, "To cure the ear ache." The laudanum was taken, and, if we recollect right, proved fatal with one of them.

MR. SAMUEL COLE, "residing in Washington County, Ohio, who was made insane from the workings of the spirit-rapping delusion, became possessed of the idea that he must offer, like Abraham, a sacrifice to the Supreme Ruler of the Universe. He accordingly proceeded to carry his object into execution, by taking off one of his feet, which he succeeded in doing some days since, in a very scientific manner, and with an heroic determination that would compare with the self-sacrificing deeds done in the earlier ages. His family, fearing that some other of his limbs might be demanded in a like cause, had him conveyed to the Lunatic Asylum at Columbus, where he is now in the enjoyment of as much liberty as the nature of his disease will warrant."—*Register, Phila., Feb.* 28, 1853.

A correspondent of the *Puritan Recorder*, in 1852, supposed to have been Dr. Enoch Pond, of Bangor, Me., said: "Only a few days ago the papers gave an account of a man in Barre, Mass., who had been much given to the rappings and other spiritual manifestations, who became a raving maniac, threatened the life of his family, and was committed to the Lunatic Asylum near Worcester. He was led to attempt the life of his family in obedience to a supposed revelation from the spirit-world."

ALMIRA BEZELY, a medium, in Providence, R. I., predicted that her infant brother would die at a specified time, and then bought arsenic, with which she poisoned him ! On her trial for murder, *Samuel B. Holliday* testified : "It was in evidence before the [coroner's] jury, that the death of the child was predicted by the rappings. My impression is that the child died at about the time predicted. I do not think she could have committed the crime without this influence."—*Providence Journal,* October 22, 1851.

This case illustrates the mode by which the spirits sometimes verify their predictions !

MR. BRITTAN says ; "Under the head of 'Spiritual Diabolism,' an exchange paper has the following : 'The spirits are inciting their victims to all sorts of nefarious deeds. Here is an instance : 'F. A. Edwards, at Equinank, Pa., a medium, thinks that one of the spirits communicating through him is the devil, to whom, as directed, he offered a sacrifice of burnt cats. Then the spirit told him he must kill his daughter and an apprentice-boy at work in his shop, and offer them up. He told his folks that the spirit had directed him so to do, and he must do so. Fearful lest he should do so, as he appeared perfectly under the control of the so-called spirit, indeed, perfectly insane, his friends had him placed under restraint."—*Telegraph*, May 12, 1855.

Is it possible that Mr. Brittan and his fraternity can discover nothing "*wrong*" in hazarding such consequences as these? Would they play with vipers and scorpions and throw them to their children? If this would be wrong, so is necromancy. If we play with vipers, scorpions and demons, we must expect their play in return!

ACKNOWLEDGMENT OF DEMONIAC MURDERS AND SUICIDES.

"*A possible cause of Suicide, and Remedy.*—We see in the *Ohio State Journal* of Dec. 6th, 1854, an account of the suicide of a Mr. Dunbar. He complained on Monday of depression of spirits; reasoned about it; prepared for his marriage, set for Wednesday morning. In the afternoon of Tuesday he bought strychnine, ostensibly for a neighbor to kill rats. On Tuesday evening he again spoke of his melancholy, saying *he knew no cause* for it. At 10 P. M. went to bed, and soon after was dead from strychnine.

"A Mr. R., of Ohio, was cut down during an attempt to hang himself. He was thankful for the service. Said he *knew no cause* for his making the attempt.

"A man of, or near Knightsville, Indiana, went to a spirit circle, holding it in great contempt. He was in good health. Twelve days afterwards he died. He was affected strangely from that period till his death, committing hostilities on himself, thrusting his hands into the fire, etc. This was told me by a respectable-looking traveler. No name was mentioned.

"Philip Jarret's daughter, aged fifteen, of Belmont County, Ohio, was singularly affected from October, 1851, to March, 1852. She had paroxysms of extreme profanity and obscenity, though uniformly decent when in health. They held her at times, to keep her from biting her own limbs. During her illness the dwelling-house was much annoyed by raps from invisible powers. A reputed witch-doctor was called in the latter part of February, 1852. He made passes, or operated by the laying on of hands. She then recovered suddenly (in a few minutes her father says,) and the noises ceased. She had been attended in the fall and winter by allopathic doctors, who did not consider her insane, but develish.

"Mr. Pinel—quoted by Dr. Rush in his lecture on Medical Jurisprudence, page 382, mentions the case of a man who had a murdering impulse 'in no degree obedient to his will,' but whose memory, judgment, and imagination were perfectly sound. The doctor reports several cases similar, in which persons apparently sane have committed hostilities on themselves, wives, or children, *without knowing* a cause for it. Whether these persons owe their afflictions to the *cause stated in the 5th of Mark*, as affecting the man who was 'always crying, and cutting himself with stones,' *until delivered of the unclean spirits* by Christ, may deserve consideration. His *cutting himself was suicidal.*"

"When one is diseased in the will, and hostile to himself, though in other respects rational, he may be possessed by a Spirit, who controls his actions, and makes him commit such hostilities. The case of Jarret's daughter seems to indicate *demesmerization* as a curative; also *that* in Mark v.; Christ in Matthew xii. 27, implies that others cast out spirits as well as he: "If I by Beelzebub cast out devils, by whom do your children cast them out?" Josephus, in the 8th book of Jewish Antiquities, chapter 2d, speaks of it as a *sanative practice,* and that he had seen one Eleazer do it in the presence of the Emperor Vespasian; and that he placed a bowl of water before the patient, and commanded the spirit to upset it as he passed out.

"As to the power of evil spirits to take possession of one, there may be causes for it, both moral and physical. Touching the case at Knightsville, our guardian spirits may be repelled by extreme perverseness, leaving us to be controlled by bad spirits, whose presence is said to be known by a certain feeling of despondency and uneasiness. The same causes that make our neighbors despise us, may make the spirits despise us, and abandon us to bad spirits, obduracy, hardness of heart, or utter disregard of truth, if it conflicts with prejudice—persisting to hold the same opinion, if convinced against the will. No offence against the Holy Ghost or the laws of nature is forgiven. Who walks over a precipice in contempt of the law of gravity, will suffer the penalty. Who retains the same opinion still, if convinced against his will, must disgust all good spirits. They cannot cling to him with pleasure, and if forsaken by them, *the bad may possess him, and make him war on himself as he has warred on the truth, bite his own limbs, thrust his hand into the fire, murder his wife and children, take poison, or the halter.*

"THOS. H. GENIN.

"*St. Clairsville, Ohio, Dec.* 17, 1854."

[*Spiritual Telegraph, May* 12, 1855.

Mr. GENIN has favored the public with some very important information.

1. The spirits afflict persons with despondency.

2. They afflict them with paroxysms of extreme profanity and obscenity!

3. Make them "devilish."

4. Cause them to commit hostilities upon themselves—to bite their own limbs and thrust them into the fire.

5. Instigate them to do violence to their friends. Instill into them a "murdering impulse," and cause them to murder their families!

6. Constrain them to commit suicide!

If this is true, we may add as an inevitable result, they "doom them to a part in the lake which burneth with fire and brimstone, which is the second death."*

Mark, reader, here is one case of attempted suicide with a rope—a fatal one with poison—a death which ended twelve days' self-torment immediately succeeding a visit to a spiritual circle—an instance of "devilishness" and "paroxysms of profanity and obscenity;" a person possessed of a "murdering impulse," and the Spiritualists admit them all to have been produced by the agency of spirits. According to their own showing, then, these torments and crimes must be expected to follow in the train of Spiritualism!

Surely, after this, they *cannot complain that any person accuses Spiritualism of anything worse than they have acknowledged themselves!*

Mr. Genin teaches that if a person once becomes a devotee to "good spirits," and does not obey them in all things like a faithful idolator, they will "despise and abandon" him to evil spirits to be ruined at once!

If this is true, the Spiritualist is in a sad predicament, and the only safe course is to shun the spirits altogether. If he holds intercourse with the "good spirits," and obeys them, he is condemned by the Bible as a necromancer. If after yielding to their control he disobeys their commands, they will hand him over "to be controlled by bad spirits," who will "*possess him, and make him war on him-*

* Rev. 21: 8.

MODERN DEMONIACS.

SPIRIT-RAPPING AND TABLE-TIPPING. INFLUENCE OF PROFESSOR HARE'S "IMMORTAL ADVISERS." INEVITABLE CONSEQUENCES OF SPIRITUALISM,—*See pages* 211, 212.

self, bite his own limbs, thrust his hands into the fire, murder his wife and children, and commit suicide"!

Spiritualists may cease from all further charges as to "the intolerance of Jehovah."

If this treatment is to expected at the hands of their "good spirits," may we be saved from the tender mercies of their "bad ones," which according to Mr. Fishbough, have been let loose "to give the world an idea of the hells"!

It is obvious that those most horrible murders recently committed in Connecticut by the Wakemanites, were the result of intercourse with spirits, and that the chief actors were demoniacs. In the first case, it was agreed that Mr. Matthews, the victim, "had a bad spirit," that he came to Mrs. Wakeman's house, "with his hands tied to get rid of his bad spirit," that "he was hurting her with his bad spirit," that "he wanted the evil spirit out, and said 'you had better kill me,' that Uncle Sammy said 'We had better take a stick and knock this evil spirit out of him,'" that "Mrs. Hersey said, 'the witch-hazel stick was better than any other,'" that Mr. Jackson "believed that witch-hazel would keep away evil spirits; that they gave him a walking stick of witch-hazel to keep away the evil spirit," that he "told Mr. Sly that he had better strike Matthews only one blow, and that might break the 'power.'" Mr. Sly, like all demoniacs, "appeared extremely nervous. He said 'I cut this witch-hazel stick about two weeks ago ; I believe there is great power in the hazel ; thought I might drive out the evil spirit, and break the enchantment by tea made of the bark ; I struck Mr. Matthews on the right temple with this stick ; he fell down and did not say a word ; I struck him several times after he was down ; I did this for fear he would cast his *evil spirit* on my sister ; I held up his head and cut his throat several times, and stabbed the fork into his breast several times. *The influence I was under led me to do this ; I was influenced by a wrong Spirit to go further than I had anticipated, or had any idea of."—Daily Tribune, December* 28, 1855.

On the 31st of December, Mr. Charles Sandford, another demoniac, "*who had formerly attended the meetings of the Wakemanites,*" murdered Messrs. Enoch Sperry and Ichabod Umberfield, of Woodbridge, Conn.

Here then we have the ripe fruit of Spiritualism —the inevitable consequences of intercourse with demons. It is obvious that these Wakemanites were conjurers, dealers with familiar spirits, and students of witchcraft. The conduct of Mr. Matthews shows that he was a demoniac, as himself and all the parties believed. Mr. Sly believed himself to be a *demoniac ;* in accordance with this belief, he proved himself to be a follower of him who was a murderer from the beginning.

CHAPTER XV.

THE WORK OF SPIRITUALISM IS ANTI-CHRISTIAN.

"But Elymus the sorcerer withstood them, seeking to turn away the deputy from the faith."—ACTS xiii: 8.

"Now, as Jannes and Jambres withstood Moses, so do these resist the truth."—2 TIM. iii: 8.

THE mission of spiritualism is emphatically one of deception. The fulfillment of this mission involves, as a *specific work*, opposition to the claims of Christ, the Bible, and Christianity. This work is prosecuted in almost every conceivable form.

To commence at the head and front of this offending, spiritualism denies that Jesus Christ was what he declared himself to be—"*The Son of God.*" The Bible teaches that Christ was begotten by the Holy Spirit, hence in his humanity he was the Son of God.

"And the angel answered and said unto her, The Holy Ghost shall come upon thee, and the power of the Highest shall overshadow thee, *therefore also that holy thing which shall be born of thee shall be called the Son of God.*"—Luke 1: 35.

Here is a plain statement of the origin of the Man Christ Jesus—"The *only* begotten Son of

God." He sustained the truth of this statement saying, "*I am the Son of God.*"*

It is well known that spiritualists generally deny that Christ was begotten by the Holy Spirit; they deny that he was the Son of God any more than any other person.

Mr. Boynton, of Waterford, N. Y., represents John Wesley to have used his hand to write the following: "It has been supposed and believed that Jesus was all of God, and also a perfect man, which thing is false. Jesus was a great and good man, but there was nothing more miraculous about his conception, birth, life, and teachings, than any good man. Jesus never taught people to pay divine homage to him; he never taught that he was the Son of God, except in the sense in which other men might be the sons of God."—*Unfoldings*, p. 7.

A spirit pretending to be the Apostle Paul, speaking through A. W. Hoar, says: "God adopted him as his son from his birth, as he would every individual who should walk in the path that Christ walked in from his birth."—*The Bible as a Book*, p. 22.

"What is the meaning of the word Christ? 'Tis not, as is generally supposed, the Son of the Creator of all things. Any just and perfect being is Christ. . . . The miraculous conception of Christ is merely a fable."—*Spirit of Elias Hicks.—Telegraph*, No. 37.†

Here, then, we have the doctrine of these de-

* John 10: 36. † Spirit Rappings Unveiled, p. 85.

mons. They know very well that the most direct mode of assailing Christianity is to represent its founder to have been an impostor! They very well understand that whoever believes that Jesus Christ was not "*The only begotten Son of God,*" must believe that he was a deceiver, and that the Bible is made up of lies! By assailing this doctrine they strike at the very *vitals* of Christianity. No man *can* be a Christian who does this.

This is the same point of doctrine which Beelzebub contested with Christ—these demons teach the same as their prince! Said Satan: "*If thou be the Son of God*, command that these stones be made bread." "And he brought him to Jerusalem, and set him on a pinnacle of the temple, and said unto him, *If thou be the Son of God.* cast thyself down from hence."—Luke iv: 3, 9.

This contest has been revived, another war has been commenced against this faith, and spiritualism is doing the work of Satan.

Apostles Deceivers.

R. P. Ambler, medium for the "spirits of the sixth circle," says in the "*Spiritual Teacher:*" "The spirits would therefore speak in the outset of the real origin of the book which is reverenced as the word of God. . . Far back in the depths of humanity's history, there lived individuals who were morally and spiritually advanced beyond the medium development of the age in which they lived. . .

The spirits have reference to the persons mentioned in the Old and New Testaments; such, for example, as Isaiah, Jeremiah, Christ, Paul, and John. Those persons were seers and prophets. In their systems dwelt that peculiar essence of spiritual life which prepared them for an intercourse with the dwellers of the second sphere; they were unconscious of this truth, and knew not the source of their inspiration; they naturally ascribed the impressions which they received to the direct agency of the Supreme Being, and really imagined that they wrote and spake as they were dictated by the Deity himself. . . The seers and prophets, whose names are mentioned in the Primitive History, were mediums. . . It was in this manner that the writings of the Bible, which have been properly termed the Scriptures, were originated. . . Therefore will the spirits assure the world that the Bible is not the direct word of God. . . The spirits would claim the authorship of these records as they were primarily given to the world."

Thus the spirits *deny* the agency of the Holy Spirit in the inspiration of the prophets. They wish all the honor for themselves.

Their followers teach that the sacred writers were inspired by departed spirits.

J. H. Fowler has published a pamphlet in which he attempts to show that the demoniac miracles of these times are identical in origin and character with those wrought by Christ and the Apostles.

He sneers at the idea of the miraculous conception of Christ, rejects the record of the resurrection of Lazarus, as a "big story," and gravely concludes "that whatever may have been the moving cause in the early Christian manifestations, the *same* cause is now operating to produce similar phenomena."*

Professor Brittan confounds the inspiration of the sacred writers with demoniac possessions, and for aught that appears to the contrary, would have us believe that they were inspired by demons! He says: "Some of the inspired words of Jesus are recorded, and the Evangelists have given us an account of the sayings and doings of the apostles. The Spiritual phenomena through Peter, Paul and John are briefly described; but what do we know of the manifestations through the mass of ancient Jewish mediæ? Great numbers were subject to the influence of spirits, but the New Testament is silent respecting the details of their experience. . . Mary Magdalene was a medium for seven spirits of a low order, but we have no circumstantial account of the phenomena exhibited in her case. We are, however, informed that the "legion" of demons troubled a certain man who was accustomed to dwell among "the tombs," but about all that we know respecting their manifestations is, that they imparted to the man a preternatural power, so that no chains or fetters could bind him."†

* Essay, p. 92. † Review of Beecher, pp. 75, 76, 77.

We heard the Rev. Uriah Clark, in a lecture in Brooklyn, make what he appeared to deem a successful attempt to prove that God's prophets were inspired by the spirits of dead men. Said he: "It is written of John the Baptist, 'He shall go before him in the spirit and power of Elias.' *What!* In the spirit and power of a *dead man?* Yes, in the spirit and power of a *dead man!*" Unfortunately for Mr. Clark's only argument, Elias was *translated!* He never was *"a dead man"!!** The angel obviously meant that the character and work of John, would be analogous to the character and work of Elias.†

Mr. Clark in attempting to show that the same miracles could be performed by the aid of departed spirits, which were wrought by the Apostles, endeavored to prove that devils had been cast out by their assistance. Said he, "On one occasion the Apostles said to Jesus: 'Master, we saw one casting out devils in *another name,* and we forbade him because he cast them not out *in thy name.*' He was casting out devils in *another name,*" said Mr. Clark. The truth is, "John said, 'Master, we saw one casting out devils *in thy name;* and we forbade him, because he *followeth not with us.*'"‡ What expounders these mediums are?

Alfred Cridge, a medium, says: "that all of the signs which Christ said should be performed by

* 2 Kin. 2: 11. † Luke 1: 17. ‡ Luke 9: 49.

the Apostles—except serpent handling—have followed, and do follow, modern Spiritualists." He adds: "Where is the impropriety of attributing them to the *same cause?* *Objection.*—They are demoniac. *Answer.*—That many of them proceed from low spirits is granted."* Mr. Cridge grants that many of these signs are performed by "*low spirits,*" but he can see no impropriety in attributing them to the "*same cause*" with the miracles of the Apostles! The Apostles professed to be inspired to prophesy, and endowed with power to work miracles, by "that *one* and the *self-same spirit,*"—"*The Spirit of the living God.*"† But these Spiritualists contend that they were assisted by the spirits of dead men—even "low spirits!" They degrade them by representing them to have been necromancers, mediums and sorcerers. *They even make out that they were liars, impostors, and deceivers of the very worst character, in representing themselves to have been inspired and endowed by that one Holy Spirit of God—when inspired and assisted by the spirits of dead men!*

Developing Mediums.

Developing Mediums are engaged in effecting demoniac possessions.

Christ gave his disciples power and authority over *all* demons, with the express command to "*cast*

* Epitome, p 91. † 1 Cor. 12: 11. 2 Cor. 3: 3.

them out." * These mediums are casting them *in* ! The following are specimens of the advertisements in the *Spiritual Telegraph* and other papers.

"MISS A. SEABRING, Tipping, Rapping, Writing, Seeing, Personating and Speaking Medium, assisted by two other ladies, will hold Test Circles daily, at No. — Broadway. They will also hold Circles for the *Development of Mediums.*"

"C. HUGHES, Medium for Test Personations, by which the actual presence of the departed can be realized. *Developing Mediums* can be seen at his office."

So here is one of the same stamp with the Witch of Endor. Said she: "Whom shall I bring up unto thee?" "The *actual presence* of the departed can be realized," says Mr. Hughes.

They compare this work of developing mediums to that of *breaking colts!* A Philadelphia correspondent writes to the *Telegraph*: "Have you any drawbacks in New York? We have. The meetings held at Jefferson Hall, third story, are in the judgment of many doing great damage in the way of exciting ridicule. I was there on several occasions. After sitting awhile, a female voice screamed out rudely, 'Sing.' After this request was complied with, a stout man (medium) arose and exhibited a mediumship about one-eighth developed: said but little, and *fell* heavily to his seat. Then another arose, and displaying about the same amount of

* Luke 9: 1. Matt. 10: 1.

semi-development, fell led-like into his seat. Here arose a third; commenced vociferating as if he was going to say something, but resumed his seat without fulfilling our anticipations. One declared that such a thing as a disembodied spirit never spoke through a medium. Another denied this strange assertion. One represented the Bible as *the* book; another denounced the previous spirit as a bigot. A female spoke often in a wandering way, accompanying her speech with the most strange twisting, straining action imaginable, giving strangers to suppose she had been indulging in bad liquor. These exhibitions, strange to say, are *public*. The meetings are sometimes crowded with a giggling, mirth-seeking audience. It is doing great injury to the cause, as it is seized upon by the enemies of the cause as an instrument of ridicule, when all other means fail. The brethren who have it in charge should at once close this *public* exhibition. It might be proper enough to encourage medium-training like this *privately*, but to exhibit to skeptics these *unbroken colts* is highly imprudent."

All "proper enough" to make demoniacs and false prophets "*privately! But to exhibit to skeptics these* UNBROKEN COLTS, *is highly imprudent*"! No doubt it is! For an *evil work*, darkness is doubtless preferable! The members of this medium-training family are becoming very numerous. Since so large a number are anxious to be possessed of demons, it has become a lucrative employment: hence many follow the business as a regular profession. We heard a lady complain that the spirits had promised many times within a year to make a medium of her; but that they had "fibbed every time;" nevertheless she "knew of no earthly sacrifice which she would not willingly make, if she could only become a medium"!

Christ directed his disciples to cast out *all* demons without distinction or exception. Spiritualists are laboring to get them *in!* Mediums make a regular business of effecting demoniac possessions!—doing the same work which Christ engaged in *un*doing.

A spirit purporting to be the spirit of a departed son of Adin Ballou, in answer to the question, by his father, "Can you describo how you are able to write through a medium?" says, "I feel as though I enter into her for the time being, or as if my spirit entered into her. I am disencumbered of my spiritual form, and take hers. More than one spirit can enter the medium at once. The mediums all go into the trance by means of several spirits entering the body at one time."—*Spiritual Telegraph*, May 8, 1852.

J. F. WHITNEY advertises that "at the solicitation of many believers in spiritualism, he will continue to form Circles for the Development of Mediums." It seems that "*many*" are anxious that all should possess familiar spirits who desire them; hence Mr. Whitney will "*continue*" his business.

J. MAYHEW "will hold Circles for development two evenings each week. Terms—For each circle during twelve weeks, five dollars—in advance, or fifty cents admission to each circle."

Five dollars! for getting a demon into a man! "Advance" payment is now required in consequence of the danger that subjects will become *mad*, and that the demons will repudiate the debt, as none of their contracting.

REV. URIAH CLARK advertises, as the price of membership to his "Classes for Spiritual Development, $10."

CHRIST said: "I cast *out* demons, and I *do cures*."* These cast *in* demons and *induce diseases*. Mr. BRITTAN says: "If it be a fact that *spirits, whose influence is unfavorable to the health and happiness of the medium, do sometimes influence men in the body, as Mr. Beecher has most clearly shown*, it may be proper to dissipate that influence by such modes as shall prove to be most successful." He admits that it is proper to cast out demons "to afford relief in *such* cases, though it may be conceded that the methods already adopted are exceedingly crude and imperfect."† It seems from this that spirits produce disease and destroy happiness, that spiritualists have attempted to eject them and met with difficulty! "*The methods already adopted are exceedinglg crude and imperfect.*"

They evidently are becoming alarmed in appre-

* Luke xiii: 32. † Review of Beecher, p. 25.

hension of much trouble from these demons. "*Let us pray that there may be some one raised up amongst us who shall be endowed with power to cast out the unclean spirits!*" says "Amherst."*

Mr. Brittan appears to think that ministers of the gospel should assist them in this difficulty. He says: "The great Master gave his disciples power over unclean spirits, commanding them to exercise it in the deliverance of those who were infested by them; and so long as the early ministers of the gospel were faithful to their office and principles, their triumph was sure in every conflict with the interior powers of evil. And allow us to say kindly, yet in all frankness, clergymen, that if you had not sadly degenerated from your ancestors in the ministerial family, you would have the power and the willingness to do the same thing now."†

Does Mr. Brittan suppose that ministers of the Gospel will leave their parishes and follow these demoniac-makers over the country and undo their wicked work "willingly?" We contend that he has no right to expect any such thing, that those who get the unclean spirits *in* ought to be able to get them *out*. If they cannot do this, let them quit their "developing" at once.

Crusade against Christianity.

Between the prophets and people of God on the one hand, and the prophets and devotees of demons

* Telegraph, No. 182. † Telegraph, Aug. 5, 1854.

on the other, a marked animosity has ever existed, and sometimes, open hostility. The Egyptian sorcerers withstood Moses to their utmost. Balaam went out to curse Israel. He devised means by which they were ensnared, and twenty-four thousand fell. Eight hundred and fifty prophets of Baal were opposed to Elijah on Mount Carmel. Four hundred of Baal's prophets opposed Micaiah in the presence of Ahab and Jehosaphat. One of them "came near, and smote Micaiah upon the cheek."

When Paul and his associates "had gone through the isle unto Paphos, they found a certain sorcerer, a false prophet, a Jew, whose name was Bar-jesus: Which was with the deputy of the country, Sergius Paulus, a prudent man; who called for Barnabas and Saul, and desired to hear the word of God. But Elymas the sorcerer (for so is his name by interpretation) withstood them, seeking to turn away the deputy from the faith. Then Saul, who also *is called* Paul, filled with the Holy Ghost, set his eyes on him, and said, O full of all subtilty and all mischief, *thou* child of the devil, *thou* enemy of all righteousness, wilt thou not cease to pervert the right ways of the Lord? And now, behold the hand of the Lord *is* upon thee, and thou shalt be blind, not seeing the sun for a season. And immediately there fell on him a mist and a darkness; and he went about seeking some to lead him by the hand. Then the deputy, when he saw what was done, believed, being astonished at the doctrine of the Lord."—Acts xiii: 6, 12.

Modern sorcerers, like their predecessors, seem determined to do their utmost against Christianity. "Can the Ethiopian change his skin, or the leopard his spots? then may ye also do good that are accustomed to do evil."

A correspondent of the *New England Spiritualist*, writing from Albion, Mich., May 5, 1855, thus discourseth:

"Our cause has prospered finely in this place for the last year. We now have regular preaching through Mrs. Sprague, of Bellevue, twice on Sundays and once on Thursday evening of each week. Our numbers have increased within the last year from about a dozen to from three to five hundred believers, and the ranks are swelling daily. We now have most of the different phases of the phenomena. Mediums are increasing in numbers and improving in development all around us. We have had a strong opposition from the churches (as a matter of course) and their hold has been strong on the public mind till within a short time past. It has recently very much diminished. The Methodist State Theological Seminary is located in this place, with its dozen ministers and more in making. But their ranks are weakening. Several of their strongest supporters have bolted and come over to the spiritualist ranks, and many more wavering and enquiring the way. I would state as a proof of progress, that the Baptist and Episcopal churches are closed for want of a support; and a few weeks since the Presbyterian minister had a sudden call to leave, on two week's notice, and remove to Connecticut, and the society are left to the mercy of the elements, with their house also closed—probably no more to be opened as an orthodox church. The Methodists have been straining every nerve to sustain themselves, but their minister was heard to tell one of his members that if the Spiritualist meetings were kept up in the Hall, by *that woman,* three months longer, they would have to close up their church for want of hearers ! This last winter they had a protracted meeting for about a week, every night. When the evening came for Mrs. Sprague to speak in the Hall, it was crowded to overflowing, and many went away for want of room to stand. Some of them went over to the protracted meeting at the Methodist house, and on their arrival there found only *fourteen* besides the minister, who was trying to rally them to battle against the common enemy. * * Light is springing up, and the dark forms of formal worship are fast passing away. Many minds that have hired their thinking done for them, are now trying to reason for the first time for themselves ; hence their progression.

"Yours for the promulgation of the Harmonial Philosophy. ELMER WOODRUFF."

So Albion has its *patron demon,* its heathen god, who furnishes the place with "regular preaching *through* Mrs. Sprague." A regular onslaught has been made on the Baptist, Methodist, Episcopal and Presbyterin churches ; the influence of a protracted meeting has been resisted ; some "are now trying to reason *for the first time for themselves*"*!* Hence their great progression !"

SELDON J. FINNEY advertises in the *Spiritual*

Universe, that he is ready "to discuss with any orthodox clergyman; First, the *Divine and Miraculous Origin, Authority, Infallibility, and Influence* of the Jewish and Christian Scriptures—the Bible—and secondly, the *Principles* and Influence of the *Harmonial Philosophy.*" He "*will deny the first proposition,* and affirm the reasonableness and truthfulness of the second."

Spiritualists denominate Christianity, "learned skepticism, baptized in the name of Jesus."* They teach that "This is the commencement of the millennium, and it will be established on the *ruins of all churches.* Sectarianism must come down before truth and love can reign among men. The clergy, instead of leading men to God, are barriers in their way."—*Telegraph,* No. 8.

Mr. Boynton represents the spirit of Lorenzo Dow to have said through him: "All Christians, or professed Christians, are idolators; they preach against idolatry, but they are paying divine homage to a created being. All are not thus hypocritical; many are ignorant, but the priests, most of them, know better. When I say priests, I mean the clergy of all sects; they are the *worst class spirits have to deal with.*"† This is just such a compliment as clergymen should ever hope to receive from these spirits.

A correspondent to the *Telegraph,* when writing an account of a pic-nic near Boston in 1854, says:

* Shekinah, p. 301. * Unfoldings, p. 13.

"The second speaker was J. S. Loveland, who at present presides over the Charlestown Society as a speaker. Mr. L. was formerly a Methodist Episcopal clergyman of good standing, but having had his eyes open to the glorious truths of modern spiritualism, he at once buckled on his armor and came out boldly into the *great battle-field of progress to fight the hosts of old theology.*"

So it is their avowed work "to *fight the hosts*" *of Christianity!*

It is not merely against the *abuses* of religious institutions, but against *Christianity as a system* that this war is waged. S. B. Brittan, who desires to be considered *the* expounder of Spiritualism, styles Christianity "*Mythological Theology,*" and speaks of Christians as "Those who devoutly cherish all the *mythical* features of this *corrupt system.*"* He says "we insist that *Moses was probably no more inspired than Louis Kossuth.*" Because the law says "Thou shalt not suffer a witch to live," he concludes that "Deity had really no more to do with that law than he has with some of our laws which are neither very wise nor very humane." He says the "assumed plenary inspiration" of the Bible is "a stumbling block," and rejoices in hope that "the reign of all such authorities is rapidly drawing to a close."†

Spiritualists wish the Bible done away, because it is the chief obstacle to the progress of these de-

* Review of Beecher, pp. 48, 44. † Review of Butler, pp. 47, 45, 13.

mon-inspired prophets. Mr. Davis says: "the seal of infallibility must be broken away [from the Bible,] before a new light and beauty can enliven and embellish the mystical disclosures of any seer, prophet, or evangelist."*

Sorcerers and their "*mystical disclosures*" are condemned by the Bible, therefore they wish it annihilated.

A. J. Davis, when speaking of the New Testament designation of social relations, says, "It is nothing less than the *dismal echo of the voice of a barbarous age!* In the solemn twilight of that age all Christian institutions exist. Indeed it would be folly to expect the churches to rise above the cause of their existence. They originated with the youthful imaginings of a youthful race—from doleful *conjectures* concerning an angry deity, and man's indebtedness to him, and from a barbarous conception of a plan to liquidate that debt, by infinite sacrifices and countless penances. We may, therefore, rest in the conviction that churches, so long as they remain *true* to biblical authority, will favor *oriental and semi-barbarous customs.*"† He complains that "owing to the dogmatism of infallibility, the Bible is taught now-a-days as it was nearly four centuries ago"—styles the Scriptures "the *paper and ink relicts* of Christianity—a foundation as impermanent as the changeful sand," and not adapted to the wants or requirements of the

* Review of Bushnell, p. 10. † Harmonia, vol. 4, p. 251.

nineteenth century." Those of his faith reject Him, whom they style "the cruel and capricious God generally worshiped by Bible Christians."*

Mr. DAVIS says: "The Jewish God is cruel, capricious, and tyrannical," whose "kingdom is more despotic, and more contracted in principle, than the present government of the Russian Empire." "The old Testament idea of a Deity is the outgrowth of the despotic stage of human mental development, a superannuated monotheistic conception." In the opinion of his fraternity "The developments of republicanism, and of mental happiness among men, depend very much upon the *absence* of these dogmatical compilations, or fossil relicts, of an old Hebrew and Chaldean theology." The Bible account of creation is "a very interesting *myth*, mainly a plagiarism from the early traditions and cosmological doctrines of the ancient Persians and Chaldeans," and instead of being "a divine revelation of truth," is a pagan relict, which should no more command serious respect than the ancient doctrines of Fetichism." They regard this spiritual movement as *the last great conflict previous to the millennium*, "the great question of the age, which is destined to convulse and divide Protestantism, and around which all other religious controversies must necessarily revolve."†

"The thunders of a stupendous reformation are

* Review of Dr. Bushnell, pp. 10, 21, 24, 26, 47.

† Review of Bushnell, pp. 61, 62, 70, 90, 3.

soon to issue from the now open mouth of the Protestant church. The supernatural faith," i. e., a belief in the authenticity of the Scriptures, "will be shaken, as a reed in the tempest. New channels will be formed for the inflowing of new truths, and then a long-promised era will steal upon the religious and political world. You may be assured of the truth of this *approaching crisis.* The world must recognize it, because it will be accompanied with *war;* for politics are inseparably connected all over the world, with religious systems. Religion will develope reason; but politics will impel the masses to *unsheath the sword, and to stain the bosom of nature with blood!* Friends of progress, be not discouraged, for the FINAL CRISIS must come; *then the strange interregnum.* Protestantism as now constructed will first decay; because it is to be devided into two—the smallest party will go back into Catholicism; the other will go forward into rationalism. And then, after a succession of eventful years, a political revolution will hurl the Catholic superstructure to the earth, and the pristine bow of promise will span the heavens. The children of earth will then be comparatively free and happy! for the *millennial* epoch will have arrived; and there will be something like a realization of peace on earth and good will toward men."*

* Davis' Review of Bushnell, pp. 187, 217, 221.

The following cut and remarks, copied from No. 9 of *Spirit Leaves*, published by the *Society for the Diffusion of Spiritual Knowledge*, were intended to exhibit the opinion and purposes which Spiritualists entertain in reference to existing Religious Institutions. The cut is a fine illustration of the *agencies* which they expect will revolutionize the world!

'The present forms of society are an Etna to whose battle flames men become so familiarized that they sail carelessly along its base and build houses of pleasure on its sides, blind to the fact that the elements of irruption and destruction are at work, and foundations apparently so safe and substantial are but the treacherous crust over a crater.—*Spirit Leaves, No. ix.*

Says Mr. Brittain, " All existing religious formulas*** *must go back, and mingle with the elements of dissolved and forgotten things.*" " The old theological forms and organisms have well nigh answered the end of their being," and "*their existence must soon terminate!*"*

*Review of Butler, pp. 61, 62.

Says *Telegraph* No. 8 ; "This is the commencement of the millennium, and it will be established on the ruins of all churches."

Mr. Tiffany, who has been lecturing recently in this city and vicinity, classes the Bible with the Koran and the book of Mormon. His chief aim is to destroy confidence in the Divine authenticity of the Scriptures. In view of these and other opposing influences all Christians should adopt the exhortation of Mr. Wesley :

"Soldiers of Christ, arise,
  And put your armor on,
Strong in the strength which God supplies
  Through his eternal Son;
Strong in the Lord of hosts,
  And in his mighty power,
Who in the strength of Jesus trusts,
  Is more than conqueror.

Stand then against your foes,
  In close and firm array ;
Legions of wily fiends oppose
  Throughout the evil day :
But meet the sons of night,
  But mock their vain design,
Arm'd in the arms of heavenly light
  Of righteousness divine.

Leave no unguarded place,
  No weakness of the soul ;
Take every virtue, every grace,
  And fortify the whole :
Indissolubly join'd,
  To battle all proceed ;
But arm yourselves with all the mind
  That was in Christ your head."

CHAPTER XVI.

LIBERTINEISM INCULCATED.

"Now the spirit speaketh expressly,
That in the latter times,
Some shall depart from the faith,
Giving heed to seducing spirits
And doctrines of devils; [demons]
Speaking lies in hypocrisy;
Having their conscience seared with a hot iron,
Forbidding to marry."—1 Tim. v. 1, 3.

DR. T. L. NICHOLS, a *Spiritualist*, and MARY S. GOVE NICHOLS, a *Medium*, edit and publish a magazine in this city, chiefly devoted to the very doctrines noticed by the Apostle as *the doctrines of demons.* A few quotations from the January number of their magazine will give a fair indication of their views:

"In advocating what is called 'Free Love,' I ask only that every one be left free to find the satisfaction of his truest, and highest, and therefore most satisfying attraction. If this is monogamy—the single and eternal union, very well—well for those who are fortunate enough to find it; or who keep trying and experimenting until they do or do not. If it is variety, either a succession of loves, or several, various in kind and degree at the same time, it is nothing to me. It is difficult to see on what ground bigamy or polygamy is made a crime.

"Of that system of superstition, bigotry, oppression and plunder, which we call civilization, the monogamic, indissoluble marriage is the centre and the soul. It cements all the elements of wrong which make up the mean and barren present; it presents a stern barrier to any progress towards a happier future.

"Marriage controls education; is the fountain of selfishness; the cause of the causes of intemperance and debauchery; the source and aggravation of poverty; the prolific mother of disease and crime. We charge all these brutalities and crimes upon the Marriage institution; the same as we charge revolutions, imprisonments, banishments, and political executions upon despotisms; the same as we charge the Inquisition, with its dungeons, tortures, and *auto de fe*, upon religious tyranny; the same as we charge the horrors of the middle passage, the possible and actual cruelties of a Legree, and the fugitive slave law, upon the institution of Slavery.

"The moralism of civilization is obscene, impious, partial, discordant, and produces everywhere disease of body and misery of soul, plunging man into a hideous concatenation of discord and crime. The society that we want, is men and women, living in *freedom*, sustaining themselves by their own industry, dealing with each other in equity, respecting each other's sovereignty, and *governed by their attractions*; no one presuming to interfere in the delicate, the private, and personal matters of the affections.

"Our friend says: 'I am more in favor of the Free Love reform than I dare let be known, at present, by an open avowal.' The present damming up process favors not life, but stagnation; not purity, but putridity. Has the state any right to make laws regulating the strictly private affairs, the affections of men and women? * * Has the state any more right to decide for me how many I may love, than how much I may eat, or what clothes I shall wear? The very mischievous error that Free Love will do only for pure and elevated beings, must be exploded. The low and vile most need its elevating and purifying influence. They are the very ones who need to be surrounded by the best of circumstances. * * The poor wretches who are controlled by circumstances, and liable to be carried hither and thither by the power of passion, are, in marriage, helpless under its relentless sway."

With these earnest *advocates* of libertinism, marriage is denounced as the "*monster curse of civilization.*" Their magazine is chiefly devoted to this kind of "Progressive Literature." They contend for the abrogation of every law which renders the marriage tie sacred and inviolable, and the immediate practice of Free Love principles, in utter contempt of all law, human and Divine.

Dr. Lazarus, who has written in favor of Free Love, but who doubts the expediency of the practice before a change is wrought in the law and public opinion, is soundly lectured for his defection.

"Such advice, carried out in practice," says Dr. Nichols, "would indefinitely postpone any reform movement, whenever, or wherever commenced. Dr. Lazarus loved a beautiful rose-bud of the prairies, and she loved him. Rather than run the risk of being sent to state prison, by any moral donkey, in any puritanical state they might choose to visit; rather than be tabooed by the general impertinence of civilization, they submitted to the legal handcuffing process, by an Indiana Justice of the Peace, with about the same respect for the operation that an American has for the equally legal system of passport-nuisances, which he finds such an impertinent interference with the freedom of foreign travel. But the slave must show his pass, the traveler his passport, and the civilizee his marriage certificate. If we are to wait till the mass of mind is prepared to adopt the true theory (which would never be, with nothing but words on our part,) they who most need these true conditions will die before their realization. Our only true course is to act up to our highest convictions. It is by truthful and heroic deeds that bigotry and intolerance are to be crushed, and humanity saved."

A secret Society has been organized in this city, with Dr. Nichols as its prime director, for the promulgation of these doctrines, and for mutual protection and defence in carrying them out in practice. It is styled the "Progressive Union, a society for Mutual Protection in Right."

A few extracts from the pamphlet which is made the pioneer vehicle for setting forth the objects of this Association, will give some idea of its character and mode of operation.

"T. L. Nichols, M. D., voluntarily assumes the charge of the Central Bureau, and gratuitously performs the office of Secretary of the Society. We establish therefore, as the focus of this organization, a Central Bureau, in the city of New York; open a book of records, and receive the names of all persons who have now the intelligence, the principles, and the courage to enter this Society. We recognize the right and sovereignty of the individual to be above all artificial and arbitrary institutions; and hold ourselves free to oppose and destroy all despotisms over the person, thoughts, or affections of our common humanity. Freedom to love those who are lovely to us, and who are ours by congeniality of nature and a spiritual sympathy; freedom to enjoy the pleasures of social harmony, and to avoid and escape from the miseries of social discordance. We have abolished imprisonment for debt; and bankrupt laws free the poor debtor. So marriage contracts may be set aside on the ground of poverty of the affections. We join to aid each other for mutual protection in these rights; and to exert our united influence against all opposing wrongs. Members have officiated from nearly every State in the Union, men and women in nearly equal numbers, nearly all full members. * * When this Society has the requisite numbers, then will come either a general Social Reorganization, spreading over the whole country; or those who are prepared for a higher and truer life than *civilization affords*, will gather to some genial climate and fruitful soil, and form a new Social Order."

So, it seems, the members of this Society are aiming for a more congenial life than "*civilization affords*." Do they not desire the life of *heathenism?* Doubtless the observations of the Rev. Mr. Pease, during his missionary toils at the *Five Points*, would be of importance in illustrating the results of FREE LOVE when carried into practice by "the low and vile." The history of Mormonism furnishes another lesson.

The originator and leader of this Society is a *Spiritualist.* It would be strange if the majority of the rank and file were not of the same faith. He says, in a recent letter to the *New York Herald*, "*All advanced Spiritualists—though few may have the courage to confess it—repudiate marriage in its legal sense, and believe in the doctrine of affinities.* Consequently, large bodies of Spiritualists are now emigrating or preparing to emigrate to favorable localities, where they can protect each other in freedom, and especially in freedom of the affections. One such settlement is now forming in southern Minnesota, in a beautiful country, pointed out by the spirits for that purpose. Others are looking to an early settlement in northern Texas. 'The Progressive Union,' is one of these associations, numbering some hundreds of members, with an aggregate property of over a million of dollars, and made up of men and women, mostly Spiritualists and Socialists. * * It is probable that within the next five years the Spiritualists and Socialists of this country, tired of contending with the bigotry, selfishness and despotisms of civilization, will concentrate on some unoccupied territory in sufficient force to organize a State, in which they may realize freedom."

The advanced "Progressionists" contend that FREE LOVE is the natural fruit of Spiritualism. Doubtless this is correct.

The Bible, by its frequent condemnatory allusions to FREE LOVE practices, in connection with heathen gods—deified heroes—warrants the conclusion that this doctrine was the inevitable result of necromancy. It is noticed by the apostle as one of *the* "doctrines of demons" and "seducing spirits." It was practiced by the devotees of departed spirits—the Midianites and Moabites—three thousand years ago. The same arrogance was displayed by its votaries then, which distinguishes its modern advocates.* The doctrine has gone hand in hand with Spiritualism ever since, as though it was an inseparable concomitant of this intercourse, and generally as a dogma of Polytheism. Heathen mythology is full of it. Its practices were imputed to their divinities, both fabled and real, who were said to be pleased when their devotees emulated their example. The doctrine and practice is conspicuous throughout the history of sorcery and Polytheism. Now when these practices are revived, FREE LOVE is honored with a chariot in the procession—all by the authority of the spirits! Thus: "The marriage of the spirit is the only marriage to abide in any condition. The marriage institution of man is wrong, and must be annulled ere the race is redeemed."—*Light from the Spirit World.*

This is the doctrine of the spirits on this subject. Faithful to these oracles, their followers are carrying the theory into practice. A woman whose husband was in California, was told by the spirits that he was dead, and she must take a certain young man for her partner in life. Obedient to the instruction, without waiting to ascertain whether her husband was living or not, the parties confessed their spiritual affinities, and Free Love was duly sanctioned by "the spirit of her mother uttering, through another medium, the marriage ceremony"!

After these "seducing spirits had entangled the young man in the toils of a 'spiritual marriage'

* Num. xxv: 1–3; Ps. cvi: 28; Josephus' Ant. B. iv. c. vi.

with another man's wife, it was discovered that the friend at whose house she was stopping "would give no sanction to the results of *such* a marriage, and feeling no disposition, as he expressed it, to turn his house into a brothel for their accommodation, they were instructed, as they claimed, by the spirits, to leave, and directed where to go, to 'escape such bondage and oppression.' They obeyed, and found a cordial welcome in a family of believers, (who, we will charitably presume, were about as insane or deluded as herself,) where they were permitted to spend their 'spirit honey-moon' unmolested."—*New York Observer*, Oct. 14, 1852.

Christ taught that a man should have but one wife. Free Love says a man may have a thousand. According to him a man should not put away his wife except for one cause. The latter affirms that a man may put away his wife for any and every cause, at his own option, and a wife may leave her husband regardless of consequences.

An editorial in the *New York Times* of Sept. 8, 1855, remarks: "It must, indeed, be obvious, that the natural and inevitable effect of any religious system which assails the fundamental principles of Christianity and seeks to substitute for it a new religious creed, must be to shake public confidence in the social institutions which rest upon Christian doctrine as their basis. Marriage is preëminently such an institution. It was founded by Christianity. It depends upon that for its vitality and integrity, and the prescriptions of law in regard to it are merely recognitions of Christian principles upon that subject. The tendency of a system of religious belief may, therefore, be to destroy the institution of marriage, even where no such purpose is professed or even suspected by its adherents. We believe this to be preëminently true of *Modern Spiritualism*. * * The spiritualistic apostles who have advanced farthest in the system—the best *mediums*—everywhere accept the doctrine of this school; that the "spirits" teach them; that the great mass of the believers in the spirit rappings accept the theory of "affinital relations" as of a more sacred character than those of the legal marriage, and that spirits, according to their own revelations, in their intercourse, pay no regard to the legal institution, but assert the right to follow their attractions. It is a well-known fact, moreover, that spiritualism has had the effect, in hundreds of places, to break up long-existing marital relations; and that spiritualists are forming associations in various quarters for the purpose of establishing a social order free from the legal restraints of civilization. But, apart from all this, the point we make is, that the whole tendency of spiritualism, as a religious creed, is to destroy faith in Christianity, to undermine all respect for marriage as an institution which appeals to Christian precept for its sanctions, and thus to prepare the mind for this Free Love doctrine as a substitute for it."

"AMHERST," in the *Spiritual Telegraph*, No. 182, says, that "certain spirits stoop to flattery to cause a ready compliance with their wishes, and lead the poor victims, step by step, to accomplish the greatest absurdities. The foolish idea, that because manifestations of power and intelligence are made by *men and women* invisible to our external eyes, we must therefore acknowledge them to be gods and goddesses, possessed of unlimited power, has caused many a fine mind to do the wildest and most unreasonable actions—in some cases even to abandon home and all its holy ties for some heaven-born (?) *affinity*. Once grounded in the belief [of Spiritualism] do not many gradually become more careless in the observance of the proprieties of life, until they *cease to abhor the peculiar views that make the Mormons unworthy of the countenance of the pure in heart?*"*

Will some devoted spiritualist furnish the public with the name of the distinguished member of their fraternity who is living with another man's wife, by the authority of the spirits, not a hundred miles from Palmer Depot, Mass.?

ADIN BALLOU, one of the brotherhood, says, "Comparatively few of the spiritualists have as yet become aware of this Free Love development; but

* Propriety forbids a description of the use made of a table, in the presence of ladies, by Mr. Gordon, a prominent medium, in Springfield, Mass., by order of the spirits, who said the lights must not be put out!

it will soon be made manifest in sundry quarters. It will have something of a run, too. Mediums will be seen exchanging its significant congenialities, fondlings, caresses and *indescribabilities.* They will receive revelations from high pretending spirits, cautiously instructing them that the sextual communion of *congenials* will greatly sanctify them for the reception of angelic ministrations. *Wives and husbands will be rendered miserable, alienated, parted, and their families broken up. There will be spiritual matches, carnal degradations, and all the ultimate wretchedness thence inevitably resulting.* Yet the very persons most active in bringing all this about, will protest their own purity, will resent every suspicion raised to their discredit, will accuse all who remonstrate against their course of doing so because personally *low-minded* themselves, and will stand boldly out in their real character, only when it is no longer possible to disguise it. *All this has commenced, and will be fulfilled in due time.* * * * Let us all take heed betimes, lest under some specious pretence, deceiving spirits, in the flesh or out of it, seduce us into pit-falls of corruption. I must earnestly deprecate and protest against this error of Free-Love-ism, which I have good reason to fear is beginning to find a *welcome among the spiritualists.*"

CHAPTER XVII.

PERVERSION OF THE APOSTOLIC INJUNCTION TO TRY THE SPIRITS.

"Beloved, believe not every spirit, but try the spirits whether they are of God; because many false prophets are gone out into the world. Hereby know ye the Spirit of God: Every spirit that confesseth that Jesus Christ is come in the flesh is of God: And every spirit that confesseth not that Jesus Christ is come in the flesh is not of God: and this is that *spirit* of *antichrist* whereof ye have heard that it should come; and even now already is it in the world."—1 John iv: 1, 3.

THE Apostle has enjoined on the Church, to "try the spirits" by which prophets claim to be inspired. The Spiritualists, in the absence of a justification for the practice of necromancy, have *perverted* this text to sanction their practices. To render it subservient to their purposes they make three assumptions. They assume that the object of this trial is to determine the character of different spirits of the dead; that this trial must necessarily require intercourse with these spirits. That this text not only sanctions this intercourse, but absolutely makes it a *duty!* An examination of the text will show the incorrectness of their interpretation.

It will be necessary to show what spirits were to be tried, the object of the trial, the test to be applied, and the manner of effecting the trial.

The *spirits* to be tried were not those who might at any time rap, tip tables, and make such contemptible manifestations. It was well understood by Christians in those days that all such were evil. The spirits to be tried, were obviously those by whom any prophet claimed to be inspired. The Apostle was speaking of *prophets* as true or false.

The *object* of this trial was to discover by what spirit a prophet was inspired. Not indeed whether the inspiration was effected by Moses, or Balaam; Samuel or Agag; Zacharias or Antiochus. But, whether the prophet was inspired by the *spirit of God,* or by a *demon.* "Try the spirits whether they are of God." "Hereby know ye *the Spirit of God,*" says the Apostle.

The *necessity* for this trial was found in the fact that "many *false prophets* had gone out into the world." In order to decide their truthfulness or falsehood, it was necessary to ascertain by what spirit they were inspired—whether by the spirit of God, or another spirit. If by the former, they were true prophets; if by the latter, they were false.

The *test* to be applied, according to the apostle, was not whether the spirits who inspired the prophets, told the truth generally, discoursed eloquently, taught morality and religion, and made pleasing revelations—tests which are now in vogue—but, *did they confess that Jesus Christ had come in the flesh?* This great question of the incarnation of the Redeemer—whether he was the *Son of God*, as he professed to be—was *the* contested question between Christ, the Holy Spirit, and Christians, on the one hand, and Satan, demons, and anti-christians on the other. As public opinion and those in authority were strongly opposed to Christianity, *all demons* who inspired prophets, like their time-serving "mediums," taught the popular view. Hence said Paul, "No man *can* say that Jesus is the Lord [by any inspiration] but by [that of] the Holy Ghost."* For these reasons the character of the inspiration was to be decided by the teachings of the prophets on this subject. "Every spirit that confesseth that Jesus Christ is come in the flesh is of God: and every spirit that confesseth not that Jesus Christ is come in the flesh is *not of God:* and this is that spirit of *antichrist*, whereof ye have heard that it should come; and even now is it in the world."

The *application* of this test, by no means involves intercourse with departed spirits, as some would have us believe. Since God has prohibited necromancy, it is absurd to suppose that he has given a command which involves the forbidden practice. It is not necessary to leap Niagara in

* 1 Cor. xii: 3.

order to learn the danger of such an experiment. It was only necessary to ascertain what a prophet taught concerning this one point of Christian doctrine in order to decide whether he was inspired by the Spirit of God or by another spirit.

If a prophet taught that Christ was the Son of God, he was inspired by the Holy Spirit. Hence his teachings should be received. If he denied that Christ was the Son of God, he was inspired by a demon, if inspired at all, and he should be treated as a false prophet. Says John, "who is a *liar* but he that denieth that Jesus is the Christ? He is an antichrist that denieth the Father and the Son"—i. e. that the relation of Father and Son exists between the two beings.

Spiritualists can find no justification for their spiritual intercourse in this command to "try the spirits;" on the contrary, they are condemned by the apostle's *test.* It is well known that the spirits, with their mediums, seers, and followers, generally reject the doctrine of the miraculous conception, and like the ancient false prophets, deny that Christ is "the only begotten Son of God." Hence, according to John, they belong to the family of *antichrists.*

A clergyman in Philadelphia told Dr. Longshore, a prominent spiritualist, that Christ was the Son of God. The Dr. replied, "We are all sons of God." "But," said the former, "he is the Son of God in the same sense that you are the son of your father."

"You can't poke that humbug down the throats of the present generation," was the contemptuous reply.

As though it were a light thing to deny Christ in all his offices, the spiritualists are publishing deistical books. The majority of their books are such. I have one now before me, written by G. B. Smith, and published by Messrs. PARTRIDGE & BRITTAN, a revamping of the *Age of Reason*, and quite as blasphemous. The writer recommends the works of A. J. Davis—adopts his blasphemous vocabulary, and speaks of the Bible account of creation as "*a myth*"—the Old Testament as a "*vagabond* history;" "worse than useless," and that "any attempt to sink the Jewish God to a deeper depth would be futile!" He talks of Christ and the New Testament in such a manner, that he says himself, "Christians, perhaps, may be startled and shocked with my Heaven-daring assertions!" He styles the Apocalypse "St. John's delirious trance," and compares it to the wild ravings of a man in the delirium tremens." He recommends the Theory of Rain, which Mr. Davis professed to have received from the spirits—but which, in fact, was a garbled plagiarism from a work by *Mr. Daniel Vaughan*, of Covington, Ky., a copy of which was given to Mr. Davis in Cincinnati—as far superior to anything revealed in the Bible, and the great "remedy" for earth's evils, by which to make "the icy poles and burning sands" "bloom with beauty," conquer "sin and disease," make man a "harmonious and happy being," and usher in the "bliss-ful period !'"

The Church of Rome has been styled "Anti-christ," but it is not sure that the sin of denying the sonship of the Redeemer can be justly laid at her door. She has been guilty of enough, and should be charged with no more than her due.

It has been left to our own age more fully to de-velope this spirit of Anti-christ, which was rife in the apostle's day; and our degenerate race is doing this fearful work.

"Many deceivers are entered into the world who confess not that Jesus Christ has come in the flesh."—John 7.

PAUL says that "Christ was buried, and that he rose again the third day according to the Scrip-tures," and that the last "trumpet shall sound and the dead shall be raised incorruptible." But in the face of such language as this, these modern sorcerers deny that ever any person was raised or ever will be raised from the dead.

A writer in the *New Era* says: "God never did, and never will raise up from the grave, a literal, de-composing body, and reanimate it with life! 'Tis infidelity, heathenism, and gross, undeveloped non-sense to believe it!!" He says Lazarus was "waken-ed from a trance!"

CHAPTER XVIII.

INCONSISTENCIES OF SPIRITUALISTS.

SPIRITUALISTS tell of many converts. To be a proselyte to demons is one thing. To be converted to Christ, is quite another. To effect the latter is no part of their business. Some of their most prominent publishers ridicule the idea of conversion to Christ ; and the doctrine is discarded by every person who thoroughly adheres to the teachings of the spirits. They suppose they have discovered an easier road to the kingdom of God than by repentance, faith in Christ, and pardon through his name.

Many of them have been noted infidels, and they are only converted from one form of infidelity to another, ten-fold more pernicious ; hence they "fight" Christianity with redoubled fury. It is really amusing to read the account of some of their wonderful conversions! They are converted to the faith that *men have really got souls! that they are conscious after death, and that spirit-intercourse is possible! Wonderful!* They have learned one thing among the many which they might have learned years ago had they believed their Bibles. It will be well if their first lesson does not prove injurious.

PROFESSOR HARE, in his recent letter to the convention of Episcopal clergymen assembled in Philadelphia, informs them "that spirits do exist obedient to his call," that he has arrived to a "perfect confidence in the immortality of the soul," and that he deems it his "duty to afford them an opportunity of hearing the evidence on which he relies, and he will be ready to answer any queries that may be made." So this Professor considers himself competent to teach the Episcopal clergy, because he has recently learned from spirit-intercourse "the immortality of the soul," after having been an infidel all his days.

We have yet to learn that their "conversions" make them any better. We have observed that those who used profane language and intoxicating drinks before their "conversion," continue to do so afterwards; and in no instance, from an extensive observation, has the writer noticed the least reform in any respect. And yet these persons, many of whom have but just learned "that there is a spirit in man," think they should be the religious teachers of the age! A little wisdom would incline such persons, for a while at least, to

"Let those teach others who themselves excel.'

The Editor of the *New York Tribune* when reviewing the so-called discussion between Brittan and Richmond, says : " We have very harsh things to say of all parties concerned, and the book into the bargain. Messrs. PARTRIDGE & BRITTAN will not thank us for our opinion of the ' better class' of their publications, if the present work is to be considered as a specimen. They must understand that we look upon the spirit-rapping question as a most detestable swindle. While we believe that many of the mediums are poor, deluded creatures, we are convinced that the projectors and promoters of the affair are knaves, as infamous as ever served out a life-sentence in a state prison.

" Of this particular work, which purports to be the record of a controversy between a believer and a skeptic, we can only say that, if it were not saved from our loathing by its stupidity, the evident collusion between the pretended disputants would disgust us. A more dishonest book has surely never been published in our country. We do not, after this judgment, expect to be favored with any more of Messrs. Partridge & Brittan's publications."

Professor Mattison says : " The two copies of Mr. Wesley's message, through Mr. Boynton, one published in pamphlet form, and the other in the columns of the ' Telegraph,' are entirely different ; and Mr. Brittan admitted to me that he made the alterations himself ; and that he was in the habit of correcting spirit communications, when they did not come up to his standard of taste, as to what spirit messages should be. Only think of S. B. Brittan correcting the writings of the spirit of *John Wesley!* Even, then, upon his own admission, so far as corrections have been made in the so-called spirit communications published in the 'Telegraph' and 'Shekinah,' they are messages from *Mr. Brittan*, and *not* from 'Spirits.'"*

Spiritualists are not half so numerous as they often represent themselves. In many places their numbers are diminishing. In their zeal for thousands they reckon all who admit the possibility of holding intercourse with the spirits, whether they receive their doctrines or not.

Professor Brittan coolly informed the writer that the Rev's. Charles, Henry Ward, and other members of the Beecher family were *spiritualists!* Probably he and his brethren will become sufficiently "developed" to discover that they have reckoned without their host in many cases.

J. H. Fowler says: "With but few exceptions, every spiritualist with whom I have met has somehow become possessed of an *intense* desire for "*Harmony*," "*Harmony!*"—*Essay*, p. 97.

The reason for this is obvious from the following from James Hall, of Philadelphia: "When I enrolled my name with the brethren who first met at the Franklin Hall, I thought verily the time had come for men, at least spiritualists, to judge for themselves; but I had not been long among them before I found that it was not only one Pope we had

* Spirit Rapping Unveiled, p. 112.

to contend with, but a number of them, and that if you could not pronounce the shibboleth in the same way they did, you had no right to speak there. After remaining among these brethren for a length of time, and concluding that I would say nothing on the subject, at least for a time, I afterward met a few times with another party of the spiritualists, who had separated themselves for conscience sake; but I found they also had their restrictions, forbidding any one to speak but mediums, and also claimed the prerogative of judging their brother."*

Professor Hare says: "The Bible of the spiritualists is the book of nature; the only one which by inward or outward evidence can be ascribed to Divine authorship." They reject the doctrines of probation in this world and the punishment of the wicked hereafter; and inculcate probation, universal salvation, and an awful purgatory after death! Says Prof. Hare: "There is, moreover, this discordancy in doctrine. Agreeable to Scripture, man is placed here for probation, and is liable to be *eternally* punished, if he prove delinquent. According to spiritualism man is placed here for progression, and when he goes to the next world, still will have the opportunity to progress, however wicked he may be when he departs this life." God "cannot have the smallest conceivable motive for exposing men to probation.

* Telegraph, May 19, 1855.

"It is utterly unintelligible to my mind, why repentance with reform, should not avail after, as well as before death, as it is represented to be in the spirit-world.

"As blessed kindred spirits all relate,
Ev'ry soul may reach Heaven, soon or late.
All whose conduct has been mainly right,
With lightning speed, may reach that blissful height;
While those who selfish, sensual ends pursue,
For ages may their vicious conduct rue,
Doom'd in some low and loathsome plane to dwell,
Made through remorse and shame the sinner's Hell;
Yet through contrition and a change of mind,
The means of rising may each sinner find.
The higher spirits their assistance give,
Teaching the contrite how for Heaven to live."

Here the Professor has hell, contrition, probation, and universal salvation, all after death! His theology is quite as delectable as his poetry.

J. H. Gridley, of South Hampton, writing for the *Telegraph*, says:

"FRIEND BRITTAN:—* * * I have recently been holding converse, through Wm. Hume, with a spirit professing to be Lord Byron. I would like to tell you what he said about the *hells*, out of which he thought all would eventually progress; though he said it would fill me with horror to look at them now, especially the *Pirate's hell.* He said his soul was on fire, and I thought so, too."

LORENZO DOW once remarked: "This doctrine of purification in purgatory, and restoration, reminds me of the altar to offer incense to Dagon upon; I mean the old lady's pipe—when it has become too foul for use she covers it up in live coals to remain till cleansed. When taken out it is as white as when it was new. The honor of its purification belongs to the fire. So, when, according to this doctrine, the sinner is prepared in purgatory for the kingdom of God, the glory must all be ascribed to the fire and brimstone! *none to Christ!*"

Spiritualists are endeavoring to climb up to heaven some other way than by the Redeemer. *He* says such as do this are thieves and robbers. In their ignorance of the Gospel they deem the doctrines of demons superior to those of Christ!

Says Prof. Hare: "Christ has no better reward for his apostles, than visionary, temporal judgeships, which neither did, nor could come into existence. In lieu of an eternal progressive happiness, Christ holds up the transient, precarious and limited supremacy from which a truly pious and wise man would turn in disgust. There is an *immense superiority* in the conceptions of futurity, given by my *immortal advisers,* in comparison with those attributed as above to *Christ.*"

What language for a University Professor! Perhaps the apostle had this age of wonderful "*progress*"—in which morals would be taught by thumps on the floor and religion through the tippings of a broken table—in view, when he wrote: "Though an angel from heaven preach any other gospel unto you, let him be accursed!"

A Bank Conducted on "Spiritual Medium" Principles.

"The Bank of Chicago, belonging to Seth Paine, is in the hands of the Sheriff, and the whole corps of bankers, men and women, in custody. This bank appears to have been conducted by spiritual mediums—the women would direct what the spirit of George Washington and Alexander Hamilton would say, as to the credit of any particular person, and the bankers would act by these instructions. When the spirits refused to redeem the bills, the holders were ordered out, and a six-shooter presented at them instead of the cash. One man was refused because he came with a cigar in his mouth—the spirits abominating the nasty weed—and another could not get his bills redeemed because his breath smelt of brandy. Mrs. Herrick was cashier and principal medium. One Pilgrim was progressing rapidly out of the back door with the funds of the bank, when the Sheriff laid hands on them, and the whole party were taken into custody for a breach of the peace in threatening to shoot one of the bill holders. The owner of the bank, Seth Paine, commenced divesting himself entirely of his clothing when the Sheriff went to arrest him, but that stern representative of the county carried him into court in spite of his naked condition. Paine is said to be a madman, and the officers of the bank, with a good deal of method in their business, had discussed the matter over, whether, if he shot anybody who demanded payment, he could—being insane—be held responsible for the act. They had come to the conclusion that he could not. A number of persons connected with 'Spiritual' circles have been indicted for riot, growing out of the excitement at the bank. The whole affair is a rich specimen of the folly and absurdity of the times."—*New York paper.*

According to the *Chicago Journal* and *Press*, the authorities appointed a Conservator to attend to the business of the President, who was deemed insane. The mediums then took the matter in charge, and avowed that the spirits of Hamilton and Washington counselled "*resistance unto death!*" Accordingly the President charged a revolver with six ball-cartridges and threatened the person who held the Conservator's keys, that he "*would blow him through unless he surrendered them.*" The President, the mediums, Herrick, Smith, Arnold, and Pilgrim, "were arrested on a charge of conspiracy, threatening to take life, and for assault and battery." The Bank was then closed up by law. So much for following Professor Hare's "immortal advisers!"

To cap the climax of all absurdity, after calling Christianity *mythological theology*, rejecting Christ in all his offices, and degrading him below these demons, they style themselves "*Christian Spiritualists!*" Just as though there could be such a being as a Christian Pagan, a Protestant Papist, or a *Christian Anti-christ!*

An Anti-Spiritualistic Fable.

The rats once assembled in a large cellar, to devise some method of safely getting the bait from a small steel trap, which lay near, having seen numbers of their friends and relations snatched from them by its merciless jaws. After many loud speeches, and the proposal of many elaborate but fruitless plans, a happy wit standing erect, said, "It is my opinion that if with one paw we keep down the spring, we can safely take the food from the trap with the other." All the rats present loudly squeaked assent, and snapped their tails in applause. The meeting adjourned, and the rats retired to their homes; but the devastation of the trap being by no means diminished, the rats were forced to call another "Convention." The elders had just assembled, and had commenced their deliberations, when all were startled by a faint voice, and a poor rat with only three legs, limping into the ring, stood up to speak. All were instantly silent. When stretching out the bleeding remains of his leg, he said, "My friends, I have tried the method you proposed, and see the result! Now let me suggest a plan to escape the trap—'*Do not touch it.*'"

CHAPTER XIX.

GOD HAS PROHIBITED SPIRITUALISM.

"Sorcerers and idolators and all liars, shall have their part in the lake which burneth with fire and brimstone: which is the second death."—Rev. xxi: 8.

Having shown that Spiritualism is identical with sorcery, it is easy to prove that it is prohibited by Jehovah.

The Law says: "Regard not them which have familiar spirits, neither seek after wizards, to be defiled by them: I *am* the Lord your God. The soul that turneth after such as have familiar spirits, and after wizards, to go a whoring after them, I will even set my face against that soul, and will cut him off from among his people. A man also or woman that hath a familiar spirit, or that is a wizard, shall surely be put to death: they shall stone them with stones; their blood shall be upon them."—Lev. xix: 31; xx: 6, 27.

"Thou shalt not suffer a witch to live."—Ex. xxii: 18.

"There shall not be found among you *any one* that maketh his son or his daughter to pass through the fire, *or* that useth divination, *or* an observer of times, or an enchanter, or a witch, or a charmer, or a consulter with familiar spirits, or a wizard, or a necromancer. For all that do these things are an abomination unto the Lord."—Deut. xviii: 10, 11.

Some persons suppose that sorcery is not sinful since the Mosaic law has been superseded by the dispensation of grace. A greater mistake was never made. In all that pertains to morals the New Testament embodies what was set forth in the law. Both condemn sorcery.

When Saul returned from his conquest of the Amalekites, bringing sheep and oxen in violation of the Divine command, the prophet Samuel thus addressed him :

"Behold, to obey *is* better than sacrifice, *and* to hearken than the fat of rams. For rebellion *is as* the sin of witchcraft, and stubbornness *is as* iniquity and idolatry. Because thou hast rejected the word of the Lord, he hath also rejected thee from *being* king."—1 Sam. xv : 22.

"So Saul died for his transgression which he committed against the Lord, *even* against the word of the Lord, which he kept not, and also for asking *counsel of one that had* a familiar spirit, to inquire of *it*."—1 Chron. x : 13.

Thus witchcraft and idolatry were mentioned as the *worst* of crimes. Hence the Canaanites were destroyed for these practices in particular. "Because of these abominations the LORD thy God doth drive them out from before thee."

Spiritualists show that their fabric is "baseless" by attempting, as Mr. Brittan has done, in his review of Mr. Beecher, to justify necromancy by Isa. viii : 19, 20.

"And when they shall say unto you, seek unto them that have familiar spirits, and unto wizards that peep and that mutter; should not a people seek unto their God ? for the living to the dead? To the law and to the testimony: if they speak not according to this word, it is because there is no light in them."

Professor Noyes, of Harvard, renders this text:

" And when they shall say to you,
'Inquire of the necromancers and wizards,
That chirp and that murmur,'
(Then say ye) should not a people inquire of their God?
'Should they inquire of the dead, for the living?'
To the word; to the revelation!
If they speak not according to this,
For them no bright morning shall arise."

We should as soon attempt to extract prusic acid from honey, as to justify intercourse with the dead by this text. It clearly shows that this work is a trespass on the prerogatives of God; that those who would tempt any person to inquire of necromancers and spirits, should be repulsed, and the fallacy of their inducements exposed upon the spot.

Spiritualists inform us that they are ready to receive truth from evil spirits, or any other source. In this respect, as in almost every other, they are unlike Christ and the apostles, for these rejected the testimony of all demons, whether false or true.

When Christ was about to cast them out they cried out:

" Saying, Let *us* alone; what have we to do with thee, *thou* Jesus of Nazareth? art thou come to destroy us? I know thee who thou art: the Holy One of God. And Jesus rebuked him, saying, Hold thy peace and come out of him. And devils [demons] also came out of many, crying out, and saying, Thou art Christ the Son of God. And he rebuking *them suffered them not to speak:* for they knew that he was Christ."—Luke iv: 34, 41.

When the damsel followed Paul and Silas, crying, "these men are servants of the Most High God," Paul, being grieved, cast out the spirit. The spirits in these instances told the truth; but the Master and the apostles would allow no testimony from such a source. On the same ground every consistent Christian will reject the testimony of all of these "familiar spirits." The fruit of such authorities, however fair it may appear, will prove at last to be "like the apples of Sodom by the Dead Sea's cursed shore."

If departed spirits and necromancers teach contrary to the Bible, they are servants of darkness and worse than useless. If they were to repeat the whole of that book, it would be useless; they could never be of service in inducing repentance and winning souls to Christ. "If they hear not Moses and the prophets [and the New Testament] neither will they be persuaded though one rose from the dead."—Luke xvi: 31.

Prophets and apostles never engaged in sorcery, necromancy nor charming. Had they practiced themselves what they condemned in others, they would have been exposed. If such arts had been just and useful they would have given some example or precept to that effect.

Among the good things which King Josiah did—

"The *workers with* familiar spirits, and the wizards, and the images, and the idols, and all the abominations that were spied in the land of Judah and Jerusalem, did Josiah put away, that he might perform the words of the law."—2 Kings xxiii: 24.

When the ancient spiritualists at Ephesus were converted to Christ, they abandoned their sorcery and made a bonfire of their books, being convinced that the use of them was sinful.

JUDGMENTS FOR SORCERY.

The seven nations were either destroyed or driven from Canaan for sins, among which sorcery was prominent.—Deut. xviii : 10–13.

The family of Saul lost the government of Israel because—

> "Saul died for his transgression... and also for asking *counsel* of *one that had* a familiar spirit, to inquire *of it;* And inquired not of the Lord: therefore he slew him, and turned the kingdom unto David the son of Jesse."—1 Chron. x: 13, 14.

Ahab lost his life by hearkening to Baal's prophets.

King Ahaziah died, according to the word of the Lord, because he sent to "inquire of Baalzebub the God of Ekron."—2 Kings i: 1, 6, 17.

The tribes of Judah and Benjamin were exiled because—

> "Manasseh caused his children to pass through the fire in the valley of the son of Hinnom: also he observed times, and used enchantments, and used witchcraft, and dealt with a familiar spirit, and with wizards: he wrought much evil in the sight of the Lord, to provoke him to anger. So Manasseh made Judah and the inhabitants of Jerusalem to err, and to do worse than the heathen, whom the Lord had destroyed before the children of Israel. Wherefore the Lord brought upon them the captains of the host of the king of Assyria, which took Manasseh among the thorns, and bound him with fetters, and carried him to Babylon."—2 Chron. xxxiii: 6-11.

"Surely at the commandment of the Lord came *this* upon Judah, to remove *them* out of his sight, for the sins of Manasseh, according to all that he did."— 2 Kings 24: 3.

Nineveh was destroyed, because she was "the mistress of witchcrafts, that selleth nations through her whoredoms, and families through her witchcrafts."—*Nahum* 3 : 4.

Babylon was prophetically tantalized and finally destroyed for the same crimes.

"Stand now with thine enchantments, and with the multitude of thy sorceries, wherein thou hast labored from thy youth; if so be thou shalt be able to profit, if so be thou mayest prevail. But these two things shall come to thee in a moment in one day, the loss of children, and widowhood: they shall come upon thee in their perfection for the *multitude of thy sorceries, and for the great abundance of thine enchantments.*"—Isa. xlvii: 9, 12.

Sorcery or Spiritualism has been Satan's masterpiece, the climax of deception and wickedness in all the past. May heaven avert from our hitherto favored nation, such calamities as have ever succeeded the prevalence of necromancy.

The principle on which sorcery is allowed to deceive mankind, is thus stated :

"Yea, they have chosen their own ways, and their soul delighteth in their abominations. I also will choose their delusions, and will bring their fears upon them."—Isa. lxvi: 3, 4.

"*Even him*, whose coming is after the working of Satan with all power and signs and lying wonders, and with all deceivableness of unrighteousness. in them that perish; because they received not the love of the truth, that they might be saved. And for this cause God shall send them strong delusion, that they should believe a lie: That they all might be damned who believed not the truth, but had pleasure in unrighteousness."—2 Thess. ii: 9, 12.

These are plain statements of the reason why the facinations of sorcery are allowed to dupe the human race. The parties forsake the counsel of God and violate his commands ; hence he permits them to learn the consequences of disobedience by reaping the fruits of the delusions which they have chosen ; and when thus forsaken by the Holy Spirit they grope their way in darkness. Such persons, in desperation, like the fallen king of Israel, have recourse to sorcerers and their divinities. Hence the adage, " Whom the gods purpose to destroy they first make mad."

When Egypt had provoked a national judgment, it was written :

" I will destroy the counsel thereof : and they shall seek to the idols, and to the charmers, and to them that have familiar spirits, and to the wizards. And the Egyptians will I give over into the hand of a cruel lord."—Isa. xix : 3, 4.

On the same principle modern sorcery is permitted to flourish. Not only do the Spiritualists commit a great sin in seeking to those who have familiar spirits to inquire of them, a majority entirely disregard the claims of the Gospel. Many of them have been, according to their own testimony, noted infidels. Such persons have embraced Spiritualism only to receive, like Professor Hare, a fresh inspiration of virulence against Christianity.

The Apostle says :

" Now the works of the flesh are manifest ; *idolatry*, *witchcraft*, hatred, variance, emulations, wrath, strife, seditions, heresies, envyings, murders, drunkenness, revelings, and such like: of the which I tell you before, as I have also told you in time past, that they which do such things *shall not* inherit the kingdom of God." —Gal. v: 26.

Witchcraft is identical with Spiritualism, and all its votaries will be excluded from the kingdom of God, unless they repent. They have no idea that *such* a kingdom will ever exist as he has promised to his people, and for which he has taught them to pray. Hence they seek no participation in it.

"But the fearful, the unbelieving, and the abominable, and murderers, and whoremongers, and *sorcerers and idolators* and all liars, shall have their part in the lake which burneth with fire and brimstone: which is the second death."—Rev. xxi: 8.

I cannot better express my views than by adopting the language of the venerable Dr. Stilling:* "That wicked men, either from a natural predisposition, or by means of certain arts, are capable of developing their faculty of presentiment, and thus forming connexions with evil spirits, does not admit of a doubt; but the true believer needs no such testimony from the invisible world: he possesses the Bible and the blissful experience, that the true religion of Christ has manifested itself as truth in his heart; and he would act very criminally, if he suffered himself to be misled by presumptious curiosity, to seek intercourse with the invisible world.

"It is a divine and irreversible law, that man-

* Theory of Pneumatology, pp. 188, 191, 376, 208, 137, 190, 138, 210.

kind, in the present state, should be guided, with respect to temporal and sensible things, by just and rational influences, the result of sound understanding; but with respect to those things which are above sense, by the Word of God, and in both together by Divine Providence, we ought not to know anything of the future, except what God of his free favor reveals to us, without our endeavors; it is undeniably a heinous sin, when any one seeks to develope the faculty of presentiment, in order to learn things future or remote, or by connection with the spiritual world, to become acquainted with hidden mysteries.

"Every artificial mode of developing the faculty of presentiment, and of entering into connection and intercourse with the world of spirits, every attempt at it is a sin of sorcery, and seriously and severely forbidden of God. It is strictly forbidden in the divine laws of the Old and New Testaments to seek any acquaintance with them, or to place ourselves in connection with, and relation to them, and it is just as little permitted, for citizens of the world of spirits, visibly to manifest themselves to those who are still in the present state of existence, without the express command or permission of the Lord.

"He, therefore, that seeks intercourse with the invisible world, sins deeply, and will soon repent of it; whilst he that becomes acquainted with it, and without his own seeking, ought to beg and pray for wisdom, courage, and strength ; for he has need of all these ; and let him that is introduced into such a connection, by means of illness, or the abberation of his physical nature, seek by proper means to regain his health, and detach himself from intercourse with spirits.

"When an unconverted, worldly-minded man developes his faculty of presentiment, he falls into danger of idolatry and sorcery.

"Evil spirits in the guise of angels of light seek also to deceive good men.

"I pointedly maintain, that we ought to pay no attention to the world of spirits and its operations. We are referred to the word of God, to the Lord, and to his Spirit, and have nothing to do with any other spirits.

"My dear readers, all of you! The great and general trial or hour of temptation, in which the fidelity of the true worshipers of Christ, shall be put to the test and stand the trial, is no longer remote. By it shall those be made manifest, throughout the Christian world, and sealed, who are worthy of the glorious kingdom of Jesus Christ, its citizenship, and the first resurrection.

"This great temptation will be twofold. On the one side, Satan and his host will strain every nerve to deceive the faithful adherents of Christ, by strong delusions, (2 Thes. ii : 9, 12.) Those serve him as instruments to this end, who, armed with inquisitive presumption, and eager after the knowledge of mysteries, allow themselves the practice of every kind of art, in order to enter into connection with the invisible world. But the individuals he finds particularly suitable for his purposes, are those whose faculty of presentiment is developed, and who mistakingly long after secret gratification. These poor souls are the most capable of becoming false prophets, and likewise the most capable of deceiving others.

"On the other side, the satanic host, incredible as it may appear, will also employ such lying signs and wonders, for the purpose of deceiving the simple. . . It is remarkable that even infidelity begins to think of a connexion with the invisible world, which it formerly laughed to scorn. 'Watch and pray lest ye fall into temptation.'"

From what has been presented, is it not certain that Christianity on the one hand and Spiritualism on the other, are positive antagonisms, as really opposed as light and darkness, and that all efforts to unite, confound, or reconcile the two systems must be futile? Spiritualism should be rejected and shunned by all classes, as they value health, an unchained mind, a clear conscience, their influence, and the approval of Jehovah. Yea, as they value their eternal weal and a part in the kingdom of God, they should shun its snares and turn a deaf ear to all its fascinations; for "sorcerers . . . shall have their part in the lake which burneth with fire and brimstone, which is the second death!"

Professor Gaussen, in his admirable work on the Plenary Inspiration of the Scriptures, says: "Notwithstanding the time and circumstances under which this book was written, and the variety of topics upon which it treats, there is not a solitary physical error in it—not one assertion or allusion disproved by the progress of modern science. None of those mistakes which the science of each succeeding age discovered in the books of the preceding; above all, none of those absurdities which modern astronomy indicates in such great numbers in the writings of the ancients—in their sacred codes, in their philosophy, and even in the finest pages of the fathers of the Church; not one of these errors is to be found in any of our sacred books. Nothing there will ever contradict that which, after so many ages, the investigations of the learned world have been able to reveal to us on the state of our globe, or on that of the heavens. It is a book which speaks of everything, which describes nature, which recites its creation, which tells us of the water, of the atmosphere, of the mountains, of the animals, and of the plants. It is a book which teaches us the first revolutions of the world, and which also foretells its last; it recounts them in the circumstantial language of history; it extols them in the sublimest strains of poetry, and it chants them in the charms of glowing song. It is a book which is full of oriental rapture, elevation, variety and boldness. It is a book which speaks of the heavenly and invisible world, while it also speaks of the earth and things visible. It is a book which nearly fifty writers, of every degree of cultivation, of every state, of every condition, and living through the course of fifteen hundred years, have concurred to make. It is a book which was written in the centre of Asia, in the sands of Arabia, and in the deserts of Judea ; in the courts of the temple of the Jews, in the music-schools of the prophets of Bethel and of Jericho, in the sumptuous palaces of Babylon, and on the idolatrous banks of Chebar ; and finally, in the centre of the western civilization, in the midst of the Jews and of their ignorance, in the midst of polytheism and its idols, as also in the bosom of pantheism and of its sad philosophy. It is a book whose first writer preceded by more than nine hundred years, the most ancient philosophers of ancient Greece and Asia—the Thaleses, and the Pythagorases, the Zalucuses the Xenophons, and the Confuciuses. It is a book which carries its narrations even to the hierarchies of angels—even to the most distant epoch of the future, and the glorious scenes of the last day. Well, search among its 50 authors ; search among its 66 books, its 1189 chapters, its 31,173 verses ; search for only one of those thousand errors which the ancients and the moderns committed, when they speak of the heavens or of the earth—of their revolutions, of the elements ; search—but you will find none."

"Whence but from heaven could men unskill'd in arts.
In different nations born—in different parts—
Weave such agreeing truths? Or how, or why
Should all conspire to cheat us with a lie?
Unask'd their pains, ungrateful their advice,
Starving their gains, and martyrdom their price."

Even Rousseau was constrained to acknowledge, "The majesty of Scripture strikes me with admiration, as the purity of the Gospel has its influence on my heart. Peruse the works of our philosophers; with all their pomp of diction, how mean, how contemptible are they compared with the Scriptures. Is it possible that a book at once so simple and sublime should be merely the work of man? The Jewish authors were incapable of the diction, and strangers to the morality contained in the Gospel, the marks of whose truth are so striking and inimitable, that the inventor would be a more astonishing character than the hero."—*Works*, vol. v. p. 215.

Whence came Christianity if not from God?
It is not Satan's work—
He is the chief of all its foes!
Demons conceived it not—
To realms of grief and woe it dooms them all!
Its lofty precepts and its morals pure,
Were not the work of sinful men.
Beyond the ken of finite mortals
It unfolds an endless life of bliss.
The past the present and the future,
Stand disclosed—the woeful scenes of time,
The glories of eternity revealed!
Whence then can such a scheme be traced?
The wondering and admiring gaze of angels speaks—
"IT IS DIVINE!"

We had supposed that our task was done; but the testimony of those who have left spiritualism in disgust, comes pouring in from every quarter.

A gentleman, now residing in Williamsburgh, was told by the spirits that he must give all of his property into the hands of James L. Scott, and T. L. Harris—whom the spirits testified were the "two witnesses" noticed in Revelation, and who were never to die—and go with them to Mountain Cove, Va., and that if he refused he would go to perdition. He obeyed, and was "duped to the tune of several thousand dollars!"

A married man, in this city, is now living in adultery with an orphan girl, by the authority of the spirits—one pretending to be the spirit of her father, tells her she is doing right!

MR. JOHN F. WHITNEY, editor of the New York *Pathfinder*, who represents himself to have been a devoted spiritualist "for the last two years, for months in constant communication with the spirits, at the head of the most extensive establishment in existence, for the investigation of the phenomena, publishing one of the leading journals, devoted entirely to the cause, and employing about the premises no less than eight mediums, for public sittings, for investigation and instructions, and this establishment being carried on at an expense of over two hundred dollars a week," believes in the "undeniable evidences of the existence of disembodied spirits," but denounces the intercourse, as tending to incalculable evil and spiritualism as an infamous system. He says, " After a long and constant watchfulness, seeing for months and years its progress and its practical workings upon its devotees, its believers, and its mediums, we are compelled to speak our honest conviction, which is that the manifestations coming through the acknowledged mediums, who are designated as Rapping, Tipping, Writing, and Entranced Mediums, have a baneful influence upon its believers, and create discord and confusion ; that the generality of these teachings inculcate false ideas, approve of selfish individual acts, and endorse theories and principles, which when carried out, debase and make man but a little better than the brute creation. These are among the fruits of modern Spiritualism, and we do not hesitate to say that we believe if these manifestations are continued to be received, and to be as little understood as they are, and have been, since they first made their appearance at Rochester, and mortals are to be deceived by their false, fascinating, and snake-like charming powers which go with them, the day will come when the world will require the appearance of another Saviour to redeem it.

"'By their fruits ye shall know them.' This is the standard by which we would try them. Let the believers in this modern philosophy, and its acknowledged mediums, be judged by this text. By their lives, their daily acts, their position as good moral members of society, and upon that we will hang the decision whether these manifestations be for good or for evil. Let them be placed in the scale of moral progression, and they will be found wanting.

"Seeing as we have, the gradual progress it makes with its believers, particularly its mediums, from lives of morality to that of sensuality and immorality, gradually and cautiously undermining the foundation of good principles, till we look back with amazement to the radical changes which a few months will bring about in individuals, for its tendencies are to approve and endorse each individual act and character, however good or bad those acts may be, drawing to respond to the enquirer's mind spirits in sympathy, who are but the counterpart of the mind that draws them, thus giving to each believer in Spiritualism, the approval of heaven, as they think, of their lives, be that life good, bad, or indifferent. If the individual be an adulterer or an adulteress, approval of their course is given from the spirit, and perhaps from what purports to be the spirit of a loving, devoted father, and who, while in the form, would have gone to his grave in wretchedness and misery to have known that one of his children could have so erred while living ; or, perhaps a loving wife or husband, brother or sister, approving of that which their earth life was an apparent contradiction, and so on through almost the entire category of crime, we might furnish examples from our own observation, of what we ourselves during the past two years have witnessed.

"We desire to send forth our warning voice, and if our humble position, at the head of a public journal, our known advocacy of Spiritualism, our experience, and the conspicuous part we have played among its believers, the honesty and fearlessness with which we have defended the subject, will weigh anything in our favor, we desire that our opinions may be received, and those who are moving passively down the rushing rapids to destruction, should pause, and ere it be too late, save themselves from the blasting influence which these manifestations are causing, and instead of wasting their time in running after false gods, seek the pure and spotless truth. . . . and all the virtues that make men worthy to receive the blood of Christ 'which washeth out all sin.' In conclusion, then, we would repeat, our belief in modern Spiritual manifestations is unchanged, save only, that we believe that evil is the tendency emanating from them, and the result to individual believers is to debase rather than to elevate, and to create discord where harmony should prevail. Its tendencies are evil wherever its influence is felt, and the only safety is to steer clear from them."

Such a rebuke, from such a source, must tell terribly against the "establishments" and circles of this satanic system.

FAITH, HOPE AND CHARITY.

"AND NOW ABIDETH FAITH, HOPE, CHARITY, THESE THREE; BUT THE GREATEST OF THESE IS CHARITY."—1 *Cor.* xiii; 13.

FAITH.

Majestic star! the first of night,
Dispelling darkness in its flight,
It penetrates the gloom;
It shows us glory veiled from sight,
And guides our wary feet aright,
To bliss beyond the tomb.

Faith, as a cable, stays our bark,
As through the night, so drear and dark,
We plough the raging main;
Faith prompts her sons to mighty deeds;
And on to victory she leads,
Till they their glory gain.

HOPE.

There is a hope, whose beauteous tread
Illumes the regions of the dead,
And bids the sleepers rise;
With joys transporting and serene,
To view the most exultant scene—
The promised earth and skies.

Thou art a buoy, and anchor, too,
While we the guiding star pursue,
A pledge of endless life;
From thee all shame shall fly apace,
And thou thy righteous sons shall place
Beyond the bounds of strife.

CHARITY.

O Charity! thou queen of light!
Thou perfect source of pure delight,
Thou solace of the soul;
When Faith and Hope their course have run,
Thy glory shall eclipse the sun,
While endless ages roll.

Thou art the bond of union strong,
By thee Faith purifies her throng,
Thy sons now rest above;
O! consolation's ceaseless fount!
Than thee, no grace can higher mount,
For God himself is love.

ERRATA.

Bottom of page 169 for "The Jehovah is only a council of dead men!!" read *Then* JEHOVAH is only a council of dead men!!

Page 210, fourth line from top, "compelled to do their bidding or be tormented and spend sleepless nights," only the word "*compelled*" should have been inserted as a *quotation*.

www.ingramcontent.com/pod-product-compliance
Lightning Source LLC
LaVergne TN
LVHW020239110826
845151LV00003B/977

* 9 7 8 1 4 2 5 5 2 9 8 3 3 *